JOINT VENTURES

JOINT VENTURES

Third Edition

EDGAR HERZFELD
and
ADAM WILSON

JORDANS
1996

Published by
Jordan Publishing Limited
21 St Thomas Street
Bristol BS1 6JS

First Edition 1983

British Library Cataloguing-in-Publication Data
A catalogue record for this book is available from the British Library.

Third Edition
ISBN 0 85308 242 1

Typeset by Mendip Communications Ltd, Frome, Somerset
Printed by Bookcraft (Bath) Ltd, Midsomer Norton

Acknowledgements

The authors would like to thank the following individuals for their assistance, without which this edition would not have been possible: Francisco Cantos and Elaine Gibson-Bolton for their comments and suggestions on the competition law aspects; Ken Wild and Andy Simmonds of Deloitte & Touche for assistance with the section on accounting treatment; Veronique Colin for looking at the references to French law; Armin Seifart for assistance in reviewing and updating the references to US Law and Practice; and to the many other friends and colleagues at the 'leading London law firm' who have contributed in various ways, including Veronica Carson, Kevin Wilson and Julia Randell-Khan.

Preface to Third Edition

Six years passed between publication of the first and second editions of this book and, coincidentally, another six years have passed with enough new developments for a third edition to be most timely.

As the writing of the book was, initially, a post-retirement effort and the book appears to meet a continuing need, I felt that this was a good time to plan for its future and for this third edition I am fortunate to have secured the collaboration of Adam Wilson who, during his time as a solicitor in one of the leading London law firms and currently as Project Finance Manager of one of the largest industrial companies in the UK, has amassed a wealth of relevant experience. He has updated the restrictive practices aspects of the book in the light of recent European legislation and revised and expanded other areas such as Chapters 6 and 7 and the sections on accounting and taxation which now have a chapter of their own. This third edition is therefore a joint effort and thereafter Adam Wilson will be the sole author.

With regret, we have omitted the Foreword, written by the late Dr F. A. Mann. In a sense, this book is a result of his initiative; I sent him a copy of a lightweight article I had published and he asked whether I should not turn to more serious legal writing. This book is the outcome.

EDGAR HERZFELD
September 1996

Contents

PART IV   LEGAL RESTRAINTS AND REGULATION

Introduction

Since the end of the Second World War the term 'joint venture' has come into increasing use. Although Berg, Duncan and Friedman, in their introductory remarks, point out that mergers receive far more attention in the business press and in academic publications than joint ventures, there is certainly a regular flow of books and articles on our subject; much of it oriented towards its business aspects and its place in the economy of countries, particularly of developing nations. Apart from books, a great number of articles on specific topics relating to joint ventures have appeared in American and other business journals.

What is lacking, however, is a statutory or other legal definition of a joint venture which is generally accepted, and individual definitions differ quite substantially. It is therefore necessary, for the purposes of this study, to arrive at a suitable definition and next, on the basis of such definition, to investigate the reasons why joint ventures come into being and in what circumstances they are discontinued.

The principal purpose of this study is to investigate the legal concepts and problems which are posed in the creation, conduct and discontinuance of such joint ventures. Since none of the legal systems of major industrialized nations addresses itself specifically to joint ventures, it is a matter of applying the general law in its different branches to the specific situations created by joint ventures.

Regardless of the definition of joint venture which is adopted, a large proportion of all joint ventures transcend national boundaries. Therefore, while this study is principally based on the application of English law, it seeks, where possible, to draw attention to different problems arising under other legal systems, and, in particular, to deal with the impact of restrictive practice legislation in force in a variety of other countries and in the EU. Although it cannot be regarded as a textbook in the accepted sense, it should have relevance to a large variety of types of international joint ventures irrespective of the centre of their operations, but it does not claim to obviate the need for detailed investigation of the applicable laws of any country involved in the operation.

In the concluding section of this book, reference is made to the types of literature available in this field and in the following pages there are quotations from and references to these publications; but it is hoped that by addressing the legal problems in a comprehensive manner and by looking at them in their business context, this study is fulfilling a practical need.

That joint ventures have been created in large numbers in the last few decades is beyond doubt. Joint ventures, alliances and collaboration agreements are now being entered into on an unprecedented scale, with US companies forming thousands every year. According to consultants Booz-Allen & Hamilton, the top 1,000 companies in the US now earn approximately 6 per cent of their revenue from joint ventures and similar arrangements, which is a fourfold increase since 1987.[1] It would appear that intensifying competition, faster technological change and the increasingly global nature of markets now mean that even the largest companies are no longer able to do everything for themselves. The journal *Mergers and Acquisitions* provides regular factual information on a continuing basis.

The basic English legal textbooks do not refer specifically to joint ventures. There are references to joint adventure which is defined in *Jowitt's Dictionary of English Law*, second edition (1977) p. 1016, as 'a partnership for one particular transaction'.

American Jurisprudence Vol. 46, second edition (1969) contained a very full definition which specifically recognized joint ventures as a form of association between corporations distinct from partnerships.[2] The

---

1 Booz-Allen & Hamilton *A Practical Guide to Alliances.*

2 'A joint venture is an association of persons with intent, by way of contract express or implied, to engage in and carry out a single business venture for joint profit for which purpose they combine their efforts, property, money, skill and knowledge, without creating a partnership or a corporation pursuant to an agreement that there shall be a community of interest among them as to the purpose of the undertaking, and that each joint venturer shall stand in the relation of principal, as well as agent, as to each of the other co-venturers, with an equal right of control of the means employed to carry out the common purpose of the venture.'

reasons for making this distinction are probably historical in that, contrary to English law, American law has in the past placed legal obstacles in the way of corporations entering into partnerships. The majority of States in the US now permit partnerships between corporations so, as under English law, there is no reason why a joint venture cannot be constituted as a partnership, although in practice another legal form is likely to be chosen, most probably a limited liability company.

Likewise, *Words and Phrases*, Vol. 23, p. 227, defines joint ventures as 'an undertaking by two or more persons to carry out a single business enterprise for profit'. Joint adventure, joint enterprise and joint venture in this sense are treated as at least partly interchangeable, with joint enterprise not necessarily being intended for profit.[3]

The great majority of what the business world terms joint ventures are carried on through corporations. The consequences of this have been addressed in a variety of ways. Crane and Bromberg *Partnership* (1968) p. 195, states: 'Corporate joint ventures are now often themselves incorporated so that the vehicle is technically a commonly owned subsidiary rather than a joint venture'. Others, including Jaeger 'Joint ventures: membership, types and termination' *American University Law Review*, Vol. 9 (1960), 111, raise the question of whether a joint venture can continue to exist when its members organize a corporation to carry out a joint undertaking; the majority view is that the formation of such a corporation will not prevent the survival of the joint venture nor relieve the venturers of their attendant liability where this exists. This is discussed more fully in Chapter 10; see also Dembach p. 94.

The changeover to a new approach to the meaning of a joint venture is described by Hale, pp. 927 et seq., but he limits his definition of the joint venture in the modern sense to that of a jointly owned corporation.

---

3 See also Radin *Law Dictionary*, second edition (1970) pp. 174, 361. For a historical note, see Nichols p. 425. A detailed restatement of this approach and a differentiation between American and English law is provided by Brelsford.

PART I

SCOPE AND PURPOSE

Chapter 1

What is a Joint Venture?

Joint ventures, in the sense in which the term is understood in business today, are largely a development of the period since the Second World War. At one time, a certain amount of confusion arose from the fact that the term had previously been given a different meaning in legal writings, principally in the US.

The first book which appears to deal systematically with what is now described as a joint venture is an English publication by A. H. Boulton called *Business Consortia* (1961) and does not use the term joint venture at all. The term 'consortium' is still widely used, particularly in the banking and construction industries (see pp. 17–18).

The fullest discussion to date of the definition of a joint venture in this sense appears to be contained in Young and Bradford *Joint Ventures: Planning and Action*, pp. 11–15. Their definition reads:

> 'An enterprise, corporation or partnership formed by two or more companies, individuals or organizations, at least one of which is an operating entity which wishes to broaden its activities for the purpose of conducting a new profit-motivated business of permanent duration. In general the ownership is shared by the participants with more or less equal distribution and without absolute dominance by one party.'

For the purposes of this book, some but not all the criteria adopted by Young and Bradford are accepted.

A. LEGAL FORM

A joint venture can, but need not, be carried out through the means of a separate corporation or other legal entity.[1] In fact, business ventures described in the literature of recent years do often involve the creation of a corporation for carrying out the project. It is helpful to adopt the terminology used by Opinion No. 18 of the US Accounting Principles Board, which describes these cases as 'corporate joint ventures'.

Corporate joint ventures are usually backed by an agreement between the parties. This agreement has some similarity with the 'surviving joint venture' (see p. xiii). Unincorporated joint ventures are sometimes described as 'non-equity joint ventures' (see, e.g. Kolde, *International Business Enterprise*; also Gordon, p. 319).

B. INTENDED DURATION

While corporate joint ventures are normally for an indefinite duration, this does not apply to what may be described as contractual joint ventures. It would seem that once they need a discrete management set-up rather than the part-time attention of the participants' management, they have enough common ground with permanent or quasi-permanent joint ventures to be included in the definition. Purely short-term arrangements, such as underwriting groups, fall outside this definition. (See, however, Larcier (1986), p. 281.)

C. EQUALITY OR NON-EQUALITY OF SHARE IN THE VENTURE AND ITS CONTROL

For our purposes, a joint venture must be controlled by the joint venturers and not by one party, although management may be and often is entrusted to one of them (apparently Friedmann and Kalmanoff, p. 6, differ from this view). A management contract may cover this arrangement (see p. 57). Having established that principle, the share of any one participant is of secondary importance. Young and Bradford, p. 13,

---

1 Adler and Morris differentiate a 'joint activity' from a joint venture which latter they restrict to corporate enterprises, but the pitfalls they describe are equally applicable.

suggest that for practical reasons the inequality of share should not go outside a 60 per cent to 40 per cent range. The note on 'Joint Venture corporations: drafting the corporate papers', *Harvard Law Review* (1964/5), p. 393 et seq., considers only the case of a joint venture corporation created by two corporate parents with equal ownership, but much of its content is applicable to a wider field. On the other hand, Franko (*Joint Venture Survival in Multinational Corporations*, p. 19) spreads his investigation into the failure of such enterprises to those in which a US participant owns or owned more than 5 per cent and less than 95 per cent of the equity. In one sizeable joint venture between two large multinational companies, the share of one was only around 30 per cent but the sharing of control was established in great detail. The minority share was eventually acquired by the company holding the majority share; the disparity in holdings may have brought about this result.

D. NUMBER AND NATURE OF PARTICIPANTS

A joint venture implies a small number of joint venturers who are otherwise unrelated, i.e. unaffiliated to one another, even if a few additional non-controlling financial investors are admitted.[2] Joint ventures of more than two parties are sometimes referred to as 'multipartite' (e.g. Friedmann and Beguin, p. 20). In practice there is almost invariably one party which is engaged in at least a related business activity, but there is no need to exclude from the definition of a joint venture one composed of two parties entering into an entirely new field for both of them, providing that for one of them at least this venture does not represent the principal activity. This definition approaches most closely one given in *Illustrations of accounting for Joint Ventures* by Goodman and Lorensen:

> 'A joint venture is commonly described as an entity that is owned, operated and jointly controlled by a small group as a separate and specific business project organized for the mutual benefit of the ownership group. Each

---

2 Ritter and Overbury at p. 605 admit an unlimited number of participants in their definition. Brooke and Remmers, *The Strategy of Multinational Enterprise – Organisation and Finance*, include in their definition enterprises where a foreign multinational admits local shareholders but they concede that they are stretching the term, and their book is aimed at examining all the alternatives available to multinationals setting up in a new country.

Venturer commonly participates in overall management regardless of the percentage of ownership and significant decisions commonly require the consent of each of the Venturers so that no individual Venturer has unilateral control. The joint venture may be organized as a corporation, a partnership with or without limited partners, or an individed interest.'

On very similar lines is the definition contained in section 3055 of the Accounting Recommendations of the Canadian Institute of Chartered Accountants issued in July 1978.

In practice, governments, or bodies controlled by them, are often parties to a joint venture. This does not present a problem in definition but it does tend to present practical problems for consideration (see pp. 18–20).

This study does not embrace arrangements such as those between Unilever Ltd and Unilever NV and between Shell and Royal Dutch.[3] Such arrangements have more in common with a merger than a joint venture and most of the discussion in this study would not be applicable to them.[4]

Neither does this book cover the situation where each party takes a cross-shareholding in the other at parent company level. The purpose of such an arrangement is not generally to pursue a particular project, but more an expression of mutual confidence and support with a view to cooperation on specific projects in the future. Such arrangements have little in common with the kind of transactions described in this book.

E. PROFIT ORIENTATION

This study is concerned only with joint business ventures,[5] although some of its content may be relevant to non-business situations. On the other hand, it is not necessary for the joint venture itself to be profit-oriented, as, for instance, in the case of a joint venture to obtain

---

3 Schmitthoff, *Commercial Operations in Europe*, p. 332, includes them under the term of joint venture.

4 Certain characteristics of such structures which could be relevant to joint ventures are income access and dividend equalization arrangements which are dealt with in Chapter 11.

5 Pfeffer and Nowak, pp. 398 et seq., refer also to joint ventures outside the field of business.

supplies from a common source. The definition is not concerned with any legal or fiscal inhibitions which may affect the form of the joint venture and which are referred to later in Chapter 6.

Whether a corporate or non-corporate joint venture is preferred is often a matter of choice on a project basis. The rules for common control and management of an unincorporated venture may need greater definition because they cannot rely on the company law of the countries concerned; but the considerations applying to defining the rights of the parties are basically similar, as is the application of anti-competitive restrictions. In respect of the latter, the ingredient of common control is more often than not the principal determinant and the form of the venture and its permanency or lack thereof will be secondary considerations.

Further elements of a joint venture are discussed by other authors. In particular, Cavitch (*Business Organisations with Tax Planning*, para. 41.05), lists a community of interest in the performance of the common purpose and a joint proprietary interest in the subject, both of which are acceptable but appear to be relatively uncontentious, although the latter is not necessarily a characteristic of contractual joint ventures.

Summary

To sum up, this book is concerned with associations of a small number of separate independent participants in a business enterprise over the management of which they exercise common control. The participants may, but need not, be corporations and the venture may or may not be carried out through the means of a corporation. The venture may be intended to be either temporary or of indefinite duration.

Definitions serve a particular purpose and have no absolute and independent value. Much of the literature on joint ventures is specifically aimed at the restrictive practices' implications of such enterprises. Because some of the criteria used in this book are not important from the point of view of restrictive or anti-competitive practices, these authors tend to define the field very widely. However, Brodley, who in his 1976 article adopted a very wide definition, has in 1982 adopted a definition much more in line with the one used in this book, only stressing in addition the substantial contribution required from each participant and the significant new capability created by the joint venture. Earlier, Ritter and Overbury (see p. 5) allow for an unlimited number of participants, and Lang (1977), p. 16, and J.-M. Claydon include in their definitions cases where there is no joint control or coordination of policies by the parents. Presumably, for similar reasons the guide-lines issued by the US Department of Justice for International Operations 'Antitrust Enforcement Policy', dated 10 November 1988 (now superseded by the 1995 Guidelines) defined a joint venture as 'essentially any collaborative effort among firms, short of a merger, with respect to R&D, production, distribution, and/or the marketing of products or services'. Perhaps with a somewhat similar justification, Gordon, pp. 319–320, gives as instances of non-equity joint ventures cases of technical service contracts and management contracts, as well as the granting of a franchise. These cases fall outside the definition adopted in this book unless other factors bring them within our ambit, e.g. a joint venture to exploit a franchise (see p. 13).

A brief note on the terminology used in other languages may be useful. The closest equivalent to joint venture is in German where it is called *Gemeinschaftsunternehmen*, but the term joint venture is itself freely used. In France, a corporate joint venture can be called *filiale commune* and any kind of joint venture *entreprise commune*. The term *associations d'entreprises* is also used.[6] A term which appears with increasing frequency in business publications is Strategic Alliance. This may embrace joint ventures in addition to other forms of co-operation, but is less precise and therefore not used in this book.

---

6 For a discussion of joint ventures in French see Claude Reymond, 'Le contrat de "Joint Venture"' in '*Innominatverträge*', *Festgabe für W. R. Schluep* (Schulthess, 1988), pp. 383 et seq.

Chapter 2

What Purpose do Joint Ventures Serve?

Generally, joint ventures can be classified in four different ways.

First, they may be related to a single project[1] or a group of related projects, or they may concern setting up business on a permanent basis.

The second criterion is the nature of the participants and their relationship to one another outside the joint venture itself. As we shall discuss later, there are many cases where one of the joint venturers is a business concern, often a manufacturer or a mining enterprise, and the other is a governmental body or agency. When more than one of the joint venturers are business undertakings, it is usual to categorize the joint venture as follows:

(1) when both are broadly in the same kind of business and wish to set up a joint venture for a common related purpose, then it is proper and usual to speak of a 'horizontal joint venture';

(2) when the joint venturers are in their main businesses engaged at different stages of the manufacturing process or business cycle, or when they are both engaged in similar activities, but create a joint undertaking for an earlier or later stage in the process, i.e. a common source of supply or a common sales outlet, then it is usual to speak of a 'vertical joint venture';

---

1 Called by Boulton, p. 24, 'single-purpose consortium'.

(3) when the joint venture is intended to operate in a field unrelated to the existing activities of the participants, then it may be called a 'conglomerate joint venture'.[2]

These distinctions are relevant largely to competition aspects but are also useful in other ways. Two or more joint venturers may each have a different relationship to the proposed joint venture, in which case, what for one party is a vertical joint venture may be a horizontal joint venture for another party.

Thirdly, joint ventures may be intended to cover the complete business cycle in the field in which they are to operate, or they may be restrictive to one or more facets of a larger business cycle, such as research and development, production, sales, etc.

Finally, for practical reasons, it is useful to differentiate between those joint ventures where the participants and the joint venture are resident in the same country, and those which are international in character. Among the latter, the majority doubtless have a participant in the proposed country of operation but this is not necessarily so, particularly when two or more mining or extracting companies join together for exploration and extraction in a third country.[3]

Having set out the theoretical background, we can now examine some of the principal business situations which can be served by joint ventures.

A. TENDERING FOR AND EXECUTING A CONTRACT OR CONTRACTS

In industry, this is perhaps the most common case of a joint venture entered into for specific purposes and limited to their fulfilment. In a period of ever larger sizes of projects, there is often a need for parties responsible for different major aspects of a project to pool resources and

---

2 Nigel Doran differentiates between an 'output' joint venture, which exists to provide goods or services for profit to third parties, and an 'input' joint venture formed to provide goods or services exclusively to the joint venturers themselves such as a joint venture to carry out R&D or oil and gas exploration or production: Nigel Doran, *Taxation of Corporate Joint Ventures*.

3 A very detailed classification of joint ventures under a variety of criteria is provided by Lang (1977), pp. 23–24.

share responsibilities. If the project is for a third country, it may require considerable local expenditure and it may be desirable for a local contractor to join up with the foreign tenderers. Points which arise for consideration in drafting such contracts will be referred to later. Here it may be sufficient to state that often an agreement is entered into initially only for the tendering stage, but has attached to it as an integral part a contract covering the execution of the project, which automatically comes into force if the contract is awarded within the stated period and the other conditions laid down are met.

B. OPENING A NEW TERRITORIAL MARKET

This is not the place for a detailed exposition of the options open to a manufacturer who is seeking to introduce his product in another territory. The simple approach of exporting to another territory is not always available, and partial or complete manufacture in the territory may be necessary to overcome import barriers, customs duty or, in some cases, in order to comply with the purchasing country's 'offset' requirements. In such cases, there are frequently also reasons why it is not practicable for the exporter to establish a subsidiary in the territory and a joint venture may be established with a local party which may or may not have a previous association with the particular kind of business. In many countries this involves an association not with a private industry firm or company, but with a government agency.

A somewhat similar case occurs where a mining or extracting process is involved, and a joint venture is created between, say, a mining or oil exploration company and a local interest (government or otherwise) in the country in which the new venture is to be undertaken. There are also many instances in which two parties outside a given territory join up to carry out such an enterprise within it. In these cases, of course, while there may be an element of import substitution, export from the territory will usually be the principal object.

C. DEVELOPING AND EXPLOITING A NEW PRODUCT

In an era of rapid technological change, a business seeking to extend into an allied product field may well find that expertise in that field includes expertise in areas of which it has no prior experience, or that the project outruns its available resources. This too is often the origin of joint venture activities which may be limited to a joint development programme or involve the setting up of a long-term business shared by the parties.

There are instances in which the establishment of a joint venture has enabled a small party with a highly developed technology to team up with a much larger party which has marketing and other strengths,[4] but even when proper contractual precautions are taken, the extremely disparate sizes of the participants may operate to the detriment of the joint enterprise.

An unusual variant is described in the *Official Journal of the European Communities*, Vol. 19, 13 January 1976 (L6), where a French inventor licensed his French patents to a company with which he simultaneously entered into a joint venture agreement for the purpose of obtaining patents abroad (AOIP/Beyrard).

D. MERGING RELATED ACTIVITIES

Finally, joint ventures sometimes arise in circumstances in which there is no new departure but a merging of existing activities. Where these activities are not the principal activity of either party, such a merger will normally result in a jointly controlled operation, i.e. a joint venture.

E. REGROUPING EXISTING ACTIVITIES

Joint ventures are sometimes used to change the relationship between parties that have previously collaborated in the same business but on a different basis. An agent or representative may seek to establish a joint venture relationship with his principal rather than continuing to deal on an agency basis. Equally, a multinational company may wish to provide incentives to its local representative by giving him a stake in its local company. Alternatively, the parties may seek to find a basis on which the product can be manufactured locally rather than imported. In these cases, the joint venture may well offer a vehicle for a variety of business

---

4 See, e.g. Hlavacek, Dovey and Biondo, p. 106.

developments. It may be attractive to the original manufacturer as perhaps the only available means of entry into a particular market, coupled with a retention of control over the technology.

Joint ventures are frequently regarded as a means of technology transfer, particularly into less developed countries.[5] Whilst there is some truth in this, it could be said that from a multinational's point of view it is another way of looking at a market extension. Industrial property arrangements in relation to joint ventures will be considered in more detail as part of the structuring and contractual background of a joint venture.

Whereas technology transfer is described above as a stage in business development, it arises perhaps more often as the motivation for creating a joint venture in the first place. If control of the business is genuinely shared then the party providing the technology will often find it easier to assert its rights in a joint venture than in, say, a straight licensing arrangement.

It is the purpose of this chapter to indicate only the areas in which joint ventures are likely to arise and have in practice arisen. There are obviously many variants, such as the case where for one partner there is a merger of activities and for the other a territorial expansion. Also, the scope of a joint venture, as has already been suggested, can be more or less narrowly defined, e.g. parties combining to develop and make a product but retaining independent sales. Choice of a suitable structure will often be influenced not only by strict business considerations but by the impact of anti-trust legislation and other restraints. All these aspects will be considered later.

F. PROJECT FINANCE

Over the last 20 or so years, sophisticated techniques have been developed to enable private capital to be harnessed for major public infrastructure projects as public funds in all parts of the world have been unable to meet the growing demand for infrastructure, particularly in the transport and energy sectors.

What nearly all of these techniques have in common is that the lenders financing the project are expected to look to the income generated by the

---

5 See, e.g. Young and Bradford, p. 22.

project as their primary source of security, rather than to the standing and general assets of the promoters. The usual procedure is for a group of promoters to establish a 'special purpose' joint venture company to carry out the project. The promoters invest equity in the joint venture company, which then enters into contracts with third parties to carry out the project and borrows the necessary funds on the strength of those contracts, with only limited, or possibly no, security being given by the promoters.

The promoters will frequently (but not always) have a special interest in seeing the project performed. For example, in a typical power station project the investor group might consist of an electrical engineering company interested in securing the construction contract for the power station, an electricity generation company interested in the operation and maintenance of the power station once built, and a distribution company which has a requirement for additional electricity (see Appendix II D).

G. FINANCING TRANSACTIONS

Jointly owned companies, which have many of the characteristics of joint ventures, are frequently used in a wide variety of financing transactions. In many cases, such companies are not joint ventures in the true sense since their primary function is to enable debt to be excluded from the balance sheet of the company raising the finance, rather than to achieve a common business objective.

H. MANAGEMENT BUY-OUTS

Management Buy-Outs generally involve the acquisition of a company or business by a joint venture company established between the members of the management team and the providers of venture capital. The particular feature of Management Buy-Outs is the need to balance the financial investors' requirement for a secure rate of return with the management's wish to see their efforts rewarded by an increased participation in the value of the company on a flotation or third party sale. This is usually achieved by means of complex share structures involving many different classes of share and loan capital with varying rights. Although Management Buy-Outs are a specialist topic in their own right, many of the techniques described in this book will apply to them as to any other joint venture. (See Appendix II E for a typical Management Buy-Out structure.)

While the above provides an overview of some of the most common business situations in which a joint venture is appropriate, it is by no means exhaustive. For example, joint ventures are frequently found in the franchising business. Perhaps one of the strangest cases is reported in *Mergers and Acquisitions*, Vol. 18.4 (Winter, 1984), p. 19, which reports a joint venture of two American corporations, the object of which was to bring a third corporation out of bankruptcy.

At the other end of the scale, large corporations often look at joint ventures with a view to acquiring 'Critical Mass' in their field.[6] Another distinction made by some authors is between 'offensive' and 'defensive' joint ventures; but the same deal may be seen as offensive by one participant and defensive by another.

---

6 See, e.g. *Mergers and Acquisitions*, Vol. 23(5), March/April 1989, p. 14, re GEC and CGE–Alsthom.

Chapter 3

Fields of Application

Joint ventures are imaginable, and indeed occur, over a very wide spectrum of business. Dependent on the aim it is sought to achieve, a joint venture may cover one or many facets of the same business operation. Since the joint venture does not by definition have to be intended to be profitable in itself, there is no reason to exclude a common research or development project from the definition. Likewise, a joint venture may be solely concerned with the supply of commonly required material or with the production of goods, possibly separately labelled, to be sold independently by both parties. In the same way, parties may have a joint marketing organization for goods produced independently. Such limited joint ventures are sometimes labelled 'upstream' or 'downstream', depending on their relationship to the parties' other activities. They are by no means restricted to parties based in the same country. Where an established manufacturer joins up with a foreign partner to market his goods, or goods of the type he makes, in the country of the foreign partner, there will probably be no need for common research and development and perhaps only for partial production from imported kits of parts.

There is certainly no need to restrict the concept to manufacturing business. The mining and oil industries often make use of joint ventures and so-called 'Joint Operating Agreements' play an important role in exploration in the oil and gas industries (note, however, the special case referred to in the footnote to p. 34); they are also found in the area of public utilities such as power generation and telecommunications.[1] In the financial world the consortium banks which have sprung up some

---

1 See, e.g. Broden and Scanlan.

years ago are clearly in the nature of joint ventures of the consortium parties.[2] There are many instances of joint ventures in other service areas, particularly in transport and shipping.[3]

In the property (real estate) field there are many instances of joint ventures, particularly in property development, for example when two developers team up together, possibly one from the country in which the proposed development is intended to take place and one from abroad. They can also arise as a combination between a developer and either a site owner or a financier who, in addition to receiving interest on his money, also receives an equity stake.

It is, however, only proper to speak of a joint venture in the latter case if the equity stake carries with it rights to common control which may depend on its size. Because joint venture has become a popular concept, the term is often misused, particularly in cases where finance is sought for commercial operations but no common control is contemplated. Similarly, it should not be too readily assumed that any pooling arrangement represents a joint venture. If there is no common activity under common control and management, then it is not proper to speak of a joint venture.

Many joint ventures in the field of property development are related to a single transaction, or perhaps to a series, but are not intended as continuing businesses. They thus have some similarities with joint ventures covering the execution of a contract (see p. 11). It may, however, require rather more care to define at what point such a joint venture comes to an end and in what way it is terminated, particularly if for any reason the development is not carried to the intended completion.

The privatization of activities which were until recently widely regarded as more appropriately carried out in the public sector, has given rise to numerous joint ventures, particularly in the area of project finance (see p. 13).

International Joint Ventures

Often joint ventures, particularly contractual joint ventures, and those which are concerned with the sharing of facilities and with research and

2 See, e.g. Blanden.
3 See Gorton.

development, are located in the same country as the participants. However, such a large number of joint ventures cross frontiers that international joint ventures are often just spoken of as joint ventures. The international dimension can arise because the participants are based in different countries but it can also come about because two or more participants located in the same country join up in a business venture abroad, or one spread over several countries.[4] Perhaps the most frequent application is that where one of the parties has an established operation in its home country and seeks to gain a new market abroad. To this end it teams up with a local company which may be engaged principally in a different kind of business but seeks to extend the range of its operations. In countries where foreign inward investment is restricted for a variety of reasons, a joint venture with a local firm may be the only entry route for the foreign investor.

The countries to which this applies vary widely in their degree of economic development and in the type of institution open to joint ventures. At one end of the scale is Japan. Here until 1976 other foreign direct investment was in fact impossible to achieve. Despite considerable relaxation, joint ventures are still in many cases preferable to branches or subsidiaries because of the widely different Japanese business methods and organization. At the other end of the scale are the socialist economies, particularly China, where there is often no suitable private partner available and a joint venture with the host government, or at least a government body, is the only available option. Where these countries experiment with economic liberalization, a joint venture with a government body or nationalized industry is frequently the only form of business structure permitted, presumably because this enables the host government to exercise a degree of control over the activities of the foreign investor. In countries which have recently changed from a fully socialist economy to one more market orientated, the necessary legal framework for joint ventures may be incomplete or perhaps the law may be in a state of confusion as a result of the pace of change. An interesting example of this occurred following the disintegration of the former Soviet Union, when joint ventures established in Russia under Soviet law were required to re-register under Russian law as either joint stock companies or limited liability companies. The consequences of failure to

---

4 R. Duane Hall (Preface V) limits his definition of an international joint venture to two
  or more persons sharing resources to achieve some common business purpose *abroad*.

re-register were unclear, but there was some suggestion that this would result in the legal status of such joint ventures being called into question.

Joint ventures with foreign corporations have also long played an important role in India and Pakistan. They are also found in many of the less developed countries which fear economic domination from abroad if they admit foreign owned enterprises.

For self-evident reasons, in the latter categories the traffic in creating joint ventures is virtually one-way only. Joint ventures between developed countries may, on the other hand, be created in any one of them. Over a period of time many Americans and others have set up joint ventures in Japan, where wholly foreign enterprises are not admitted, and it has now become quite usual for Japanese interests to participate in joint ventures in other countries, particularly in Europe – though the motivation is usually quite different and more concerned with the acquisition of local strengths, including access to protected markets such as the EU, than with the avoidance of investment restrictions.

A particular form of joint venture between developed countries has become established to cover large inter-governmental projects which, by their very size, cannot be fully funded by one government or country. The form is largely determined by the degree of governmental involvement. In a case reported in *Mergers and Acquisitions* (Winter, 1978), p. 64, the former Soviet Union and Italy formed a joint company under Italian law for the design and construction of tin and steel mills in Third World countries. In the aviation field, where the majority of these governmental joint ventures were started, a somewhat similar pattern has led to the formation of the European Airbus Consortium, in which there is no direct government participation.

As indicated on pp. 12 and 13, joint ventures are often used for technology transfer to less developed countries, but they are not limited to these cases. In the 1970s and early 1980s the French Government backed a number of joint ventures between French companies and leading US manufacturers for the production in France of advanced technological products.[5] Some of the French companies concerned were later nationalized, but that is purely incidental. The motivation for both sides to such a joint venture is not all that different than in other cases of

---

5 See, e.g. *The Financial Times*, 8 September 1981.

technology transfer, though the relative strengths are more closely matched.

As mentioned above, the specific rules under which former socialist and less developed countries admit joint ventures vary widely. Some involve a corporate structure and others are purely contractual. Some may not measure up to our definition of a joint venture which requires shared control and whether the foreign participants can get and maintain a fair deal depends on the continuing interest of the host country in the success of the venture. Rules are frequently changed, often to the advantage of the foreign participant, if the existing rules have not gained acceptance abroad. There is much literature available in books and articles on the situation in individual countries but, in view of the comparatively high rate of change, it is important to ensure that they represent the up-to-date position in the country concerned. For the same reason, this book (in contrast to Hall) only refers to individual countries by way of example, and the bibliography does not seek to cover the situation in individual countries but includes books dealing with joint ventures in developing countries generally.

Multiple Joint Ventures

Mainly in the international field, it is often more convenient for the parties to enter into a series of parallel joint ventures when proposing to operate in several countries. It will depend on circumstances whether parties proposing a series of joint ventures in different countries can cover their collaboration by one joint venture agreement (see Chapter 7), or whether a series of parallel agreements is required; in that case the linkage between them will require careful study.

It also occurs that a joint venture in turn will participate in another joint venture with parties not involved in the original one.

Chapter 4

Advantages and Disadvantages of Joint Ventures

Berg and Friedman, Part I (1978), p. 30, quote the view that most joint ventures are born out of sets of unique circumstances, and also draw attention to the fact that they represent an organizational form for achieving economic objectives which neither parent could normally attain acting alone. Certainly many large corporations will still, except where the aim is restriction of competition, prefer a viable alternative to starting a joint venture. On the other hand, Young and Bradford (p. 7) state that 'companies which have joint ventured rate their experience as satisfactory or better, contrary to popular belief', whilst Dunning, *The Globalization of Business*, records that in 1982 co-operative agreements formed between US and foreign companies outnumbered the number of fully owned foreign subsidiaries by a factor of at least four to one, and goes on to state that:

> 'The world's leading multinational enterprises are operating through an intricate global web of formal and informal coalitions, most of which are in the advanced industrial countries. These developments induce the formation of oligopolistic galaxies with the major world producers at the hub of the galaxies.'[1]

Joint ventures are, of course, only one aspect of this tendency, which also encompasses cross shareholdings, technology transfer arrangements and other more flexible forms of cooperation, but they clearly have a very important role to play. Of course, the popularity of joint

---

1 John H. Dunning, *The Globalization of Business* (Routledge, 1993).

ventures does not mean that the risks associated with them are any less real.

It is often said that a great number of joint ventures in which large corporations are involved do not survive a long time in their original form. A detailed study of this phenomenon by Franko, *Joint Venture Survival in Multinational Corporations*, indicates that out of a fairly large sample of international joint ventures entered into by US-based multinationals, some 30 per cent had not survived in the original form and, where they had survived at all, were wholly owned by either the American partner or another party.[2] An interesting overview of the reasons for creating a joint venture and of the resultant successes and failures is provided by Berg and Friedman, *California Management Review*, who also point out that the discontinuance of some joint ventures in their original form need not be accounted a failure. One such set of circumstances is the case where parties are contemplating a merger but are somewhat uncertain of their compatibility, and, with a view to limiting the risk, enter into a joint venture which they hope will lead on to a merger.[3] In other cases the facts giving rise to the original purpose may have changed. Thus a consortium bank which was set up to conduct a type of international banking business in which participants were not individually engaged in any depth, may find itself later in direct competition with them and one of the participants may buy out the others as in the case of the Orion Bank and Royal Bank of Canada. There is nothing original in this: in the early 1920s the American Dupont Company set up a joint venture in the US with a French company, La Cellophane, to exploit under licence a French manufacturing process in the US. Ten years later it bought out the French interest in return for a shareholding in Dupont. The continuing venture later occupied the American courts due to an allegation of anti-trust behaviour. This was long after it had ceased to be a joint venture.

The analysis of pros and cons which follows is intended to be applicable to all kinds of joint ventures. Authors, such as Brooke and Remmers (pp. 205 et seq.), who discuss joint ventures, e.g. as an aspect of the multinational development of large corporations, may well place a different emphasis on certain aspects.

---

2 See also Franko, *The Multinational Company in Europe*.
3 See, e.g. Gullander, *Columbia Journal of World Business*, p. 114.

A. ADVANTAGES

Limitation of Investment

Advantages can be divided into both negative and positive.[4] The most obvious negative advantage is limitation of the investment requirement. This can be attractive *per se* but, more particularly, this may be the case when the investment is made in a country with either existing or potential exchange control problems affecting possible repatriation. However, the price of this limitation of investment, as we shall see later, can be abandonment of control over the need for future additional investment and over its provision.

Limitation of Risk

Perhaps the most obvious advantage is a limitation of the risk of failure of the enterprise. Going back to Chapter 2, the party tendering for a large contract may well wish to avoid total responsibility for failure. To some extent this could be met by appropriate sub-contracts, but they will normally do no more than deal with the consequences of the sub-contractor's individual failure. Where a joint venture is entered into to introduce a product range into a country by local manufacture, the investments of the foreign party may largely comprise the transfer of industrial property rights and of technological know-how and perhaps in addition the supply of machinery and of components, with the entire cash contribution coming from within the country. This obviously substantially limits the financial risks for the foreign investor.

Overcoming Nationalistic Prejudice

An advantage may lie in overcoming national feeling in a country in which a joint venture is started by a foreign party with a local party, be it government or private. In many, not only the less developed countries, foreign-owned businesses are either not permitted outright or are subject to prior approvals, which are difficult to obtain unless there is an obvious need for the country to see the foreign-owned activity installed, and that need can only be met by permitting foreign control. Such

---

4 For a useful analysis of the advantages and disadvantages see Kolde, *International Business Enterprise*, pp. 271 et seq.

restrictions may therefore vary between different industries,[5] particularly where they are imposed administratively rather than by general law.

Merging Skills and Strengths

Looking now at the more positive side, a joint venture may often provide the best means for merging certain skills and strengths. There may be technical expertise available unaccompanied by financial backing, and a joint venture between a technically superior and a financially strong party may be the solution. Two parties may have different technical strengths, the combination of which is essential for a project in which both would like to become interested. In international deals, quite apart from the problem of overcoming national sensitivities, the foreign party may derive much benefit from the local personal contacts of the home party, which in a joint venture become available on a committed basis, and from access to local information more readily available to the local partner.[6]

B. DISADVANTAGES

Decision-making – Management Style

Against these advantages one has to set a number of problems of which joint venturers have to be aware. Clearly, joint control means joint decision-making and to many top executives the sharing of decision-making does not come easily. It should be recognized that this difficulty goes well beyond the narrowly-defined question of decision-making and concerns all matters which can be affected by what is known as 'management style'. These problems are accentuated where the participants' own pattern of organization and the degree to which decision-making is centralized or otherwise, diverge, which can lead to serious stresses, partly brought about by differing time-scales of decision-making.[7] Often, insufficient attention is paid at the outset to such problems as monthly or periodic reporting. Where one party is already

---

5 See, e.g. Gullander, *International Studies of Management and Organizations*, p. 90.
6 See Franko, *Joint Venture Survival*, p. 29.
7 See Franko, *The Multinational Company*. On this and related problems see also Adler and Morris.

engaged in the business and the other party joins in perhaps a territorially limited venture in the same field, it will usually be content to follow the original party's arrangements; but where two large companies go in for a joint venture, their reporting methods may be totally at variance, as may be many other matters, such as the extent of autonomy granted to the joint venture. Even the composition of the joint venture's board may present problems. If it is to function effectively, its members must be able and willing to attend the majority of its meetings; in a large corporation this may mean excluding its top management from the board of such a joint venture company, which may not please the other party and throw doubt on the degree of commitment.

It must be clear that in any joint venture, conflicts of interest arise between the participants and between the interests of one or other participant and those of the joint venture. Some of these may not be obvious to all parties. Roulac, p. 8, refers to a situation where one participant might look for benefits that would come to him rather than to the joint venture. Indeed, participants may well be looking ahead to what they can achieve on (premature?) termination of a joint venture, an attitude sometimes described as 'competitive collaboration'[8] or 'takeover by stealth'.[9] It should, however, be remembered that any form of partnership can be entered into with similar motivation. It should also be borne in mind that joint ventures are often at least initially staffed by seconding people in the employ of the participants, and consequently the problem of dual loyalties can easily arise. Moreover, these are not static situations, but what may have been attractive or at least acceptable at the outset, may, once the business is successfully established or runs into unforeseen difficulties, look rather different to some participants.[10]

After-effect of Failure – Effect on Parents' Image

Perhaps the largest problem affecting joint ventures is consideration of the possible consequences of failure. It will be obvious that a participant who had earlier decided in favour of a joint venture in preference to

---

8 See, e.g. *The Financial Times*, 16 January 1989 at p. 28: 'Why joint ventures can end in tears'.

9 See *The Financial Times*, 1 February 1989 at p. 32.

10 See *The Financial Times*, 21 December 1982, for an interesting example of a threatened conflict of interest giving rise to the dissolution of a joint venture between ENI of Italy and Occidental of the US.

available alternatives will not wish to find that after a limited time he is faced with just one or other of those alternatives, particularly if that now involves total loss of control because he cannot, for whatever reason, obtain control himself. These matters must therefore be carefully examined at the negotiating stage. Apart from financial problems and those associated with intellectual property rights, it can also easily happen that the image, say, of the foreign party, is severely damaged in the country in which its joint venture failed, which can have repercussions on its other activities in that country.

In some circumstances the fact that a business is operated as a joint venture may, particularly in the early stages, tend to concentrate the spotlight on it and possibly to show larger start-up expenses than would have been the case under the umbrella of an existing organization where some expenditures might never have been charged to the business. Whether this is to be considered a positive or negative aspect may depend as much on the outlook of the different participants as on any strictly objective measure, but participants should take cognizance of it in judging a joint venture's results.

In many circumstances joint ventures are not either party's first choice. What alternatives are available depends on many factors. The principal element in the decision must be the type of business venture that is in mind. A variety of alternatives may in theory be available but, for reasons of local laws, taxation, protection of intellectual property rights, etc., not be practicable. Most parties to a joint venture will have asked themselves whether it is possible for them to go it alone by setting up a new business or, where merely an expansion of an existing activity is concerned, by creating a subsidiary or a branch. Where the sole purpose of a joint venture is to secure financial backing, a possible alternative must be to seek financial participation from parties not interested in managerial control and, in suitable circumstances, from the public. Going the opposite way, one of the available alternatives is to assist the other party in getting into the business which, where technology transfer is involved, will involve reliance on a licensing agreement. In practice it is necessary to recognize that the enforcement of intellectual property rights and other equivalent arrangements comes up increasingly against various forms of anti-monopoly legislation and is therefore becoming less certain in its reliability. This in turn is a powerful inducement to choose a joint venture instead of a straight licensing deal. In practice, there are all kinds of combinations in which, say, the principal licence is granted to a joint venture between the licensor and its licensees or between a group of the latter. A joint venture in research and development may also come about as a convenient way for the participants to resolve a conflicting patent situation.[11]

These considerations of the advantages and disadvantages of joint ventures compared to other solutions have been discussed on the basis of the particular enterprise under consideration. They become more complex where a corporation is, or seeks to be, involved in a number of separate joint ventures – a situation in no way limited to large corporations. No consideration is here given to the case where two participants, for organizational or fiscal convenience, set up a number of parallel joint ventures with an overall business objective, such as separate joint ventures for different territorial markets. There is a view that because joint ventures cause administrative problems of their own and administrative costs tend to increase with the number of joint ventures in which a firm is involved, it may not be desirable for firms to be involved in too many separate joint ventures at the same time.[12] This would apply less strongly to very large corporations in cases where the joint ventures are in totally different business fields and any management and administrative problems are therefore less liable to have a cumulative effect.

As was pointed out recently[13] a company of world rank, Corning, derives about half its profit from joint ventures. The author emphasizes among other criteria that an intending joint venturer should look for partners who have similar values and control systems, similar tolerance for losses and a similar appetite for risk. It may perhaps be difficult in fact to ascertain these attitudes satisfactorily in advance. Some of the common misconceptions which exist in relation to the selection of an appropriate joint venture partner are discussed by Vanessa Houlder in 'Today's friend, tomorrow's foe' *Financial Times*, 2 October 1995. In particular, Ms Houlder points out that teaming up with a stronger partner to improve skills or gain access to new technology or products is a risky strategy as it usually results in the weaker partner being acquired

---

11 See Ritter and Overbury, p. 623.
12 See, e.g. Gullander, *Columbia Journal of World Business*, pp. 104 et seq. and particularly p. 106.
13 'The benefits of alliance', by T. Lewis in *Mergers and Acquisitions International*, January 1989, p. 35.

by the stronger one. Ohmae suggests (p. 178) that where the participants are large corporations, it is desirable for the joint venture to have a long-term sponsor in each participating corporation.

Summary

All this and much of what follows in the succeeding pages indicates that the setting up of a joint venture, certainly for the long term, requires a great deal of deliberation and attention. Joint ventures, the potential size of which are relatively trivial compared to the parties' overall activities, are likely to be denied this attention[14] and may well therefore have a higher failure rate. On the other hand, Foster makes the point that outstandingly successful joint ventures, like Rank Xerox, can over a period of time be subject to far greater stresses than less dominant ones which have not become the largest single business of both parties.

Consideration must also be given to certain matters which are not particular to joint ventures. It may be important to decide which member of a large group of companies becomes the shareholder in a joint venture. Also, as mentioned earlier, joint ventures are often made between industrial or mining companies and the governments or certain governmental or quasi-governmental bodies in less developed countries, and the question as to how the other member's rights can be enforced, in the event of a dispute, must be given consideration.

This chapter and other parts of this book are written primarily from the point of view of participants in joint ventures and their professional advisers. It is important to bear in mind that other parties, particularly bankers and other lenders, have considerable interest in the prospects and the legal set-up of a joint venture, and the existence of one or more joint ventures may well affect the participants' credit status. A detailed discussion of these problems falls outside the confines of this book.[15]

---

14 See, e.g. Hlavacek and Thompson, p. 39.

15 G. Cooke and D. Yates deal with these issues comprehensively in relation to ship finance in their article 'Legal problems in financing maritime joint ventures' in (1989) JBL 197 et seq.

PART II

ORGANIZATIONAL AND LEGAL FRAMEWORK

Chapter 5

Applicable Law and Jurisdiction; Arbitration

Although only relevant to 'international' joint ventures, it is useful to discuss the question of applicable law, at least in general terms, before going into details of the agreements, formation of companies, etc. This discussion covers solely the law applicable to the agreements between the parties and, where they form a legal entity to carry out the business, the agreements governing that legal entity and the relationships of the partners with it. The laws under which countries and supranational bodies restrain and inhibit associations of the nature described here, and other business ventures, follow different rules and frequently overlap and indeed conflict in their application, as is more fully discussed in Part IV.

The law applicable to a contractual joint venture is normally for the parties to choose. In choosing it they will have regard in particular to the need to settle disputes and to submit to a procedure for settling them. The absence of any prior agreement on the applicable law can lead to undesirable consequences, as for example when A and B, domiciled in two different countries, combine to execute a contract in country C, the laws of which may not be particularly suitable to govern the relations between the parties and may even be hard to determine. It happens frequently that the purchasing country insists on its law being applicable to the supply contract. The parties, having had no alternative but to agree to that arrangement, may well wish their own internal relations to be governed as fully as possible by another law with which they and their advisers are more familiar.[1] The result would be that the joint venture arrangements would be governed by, say, English law, but the supply contract would be governed by the laws of the purchasing country. A further alternative is to accept the local system of law, but to agree to arbitrate in a third, neutral country, e.g. Sweden.

Where a corporate entity is formed, that, of course, determines automatically the law applicable to that entity as a corporate body. The laws of some countries, e.g. France, do not recognize as valid agreements between shareholders about the conduct of a company. This, being considered a basic principle of French law, would, where it applies, prevent the enforcement in France of an agreement entered into outside France between shareholding parties regardless of the law stated to be applicable to it.[2] In deciding where to locate a corporate entity these questions of applicable law must play an important part.[3] However, where a corporate joint venture is being formed to carry out activities in a particular territory, the requirement for local credibility will frequently dictate that the joint venture is incorporated under the laws of the country concerned.

It must also be remembered that while most legal systems allow contracting parties latitude in ordering their affairs, joint venture contracts belong to the group covered by the term 'complex long-term contracts', which in some legal systems, particularly on the Continent of Europe, may imply that they are subject to renegotiation and possible

---

1 A case of two parties, one American and one English, choosing English law to govern their relations in a joint oil exploration venture in Libya, is dealt with along these lines in *B.P. Exploration Company (Libya) Ltd* v *Hunt* [1976] 3 All ER 879. This case was continued in [1979] 1 WLR 783 and reviewed by the House of Lords on 4 February 1982 (see (1982) *The Times*, 5 February, p. 19). As far as can be inferred from the published material, this case is not a joint venture as defined here since the entire management of the project appears to have resided in one party and the sharing arrangements are also at least somewhat special. Lord Brandon in the House of Lords' decision refers to it as a 'combined adventure'.

2 French law allows a number of exceptions to this principle, the most important of which is where the agreement between the shareholders is in the interests of the company. For example, where the company is a 50/50 joint venture, a shareholders' agreement entered into with a view to avoiding management deadlock could be regarded as being in the interests of the company.

3 These and related questions, such as the language governing an agreement, have been reviewed from the point of view of a US participant by Gavin.

judicial or arbitral amendment in the light of fundamentally changed circumstances.

In international joint ventures, arbitration clauses can often be found in the joint venture contract. This, coupled with the choice of a governing legal system which would be neither party's first choice but may perhaps be the law of the country where the arbitration is meant to take place, is sometimes considered a suitable compromise. Warnings, however, are appropriate: a court or arbitrators might in certain circumstances regard such a choice of law as invalid; and even more seriously, it may – if upheld – lead to quite unintended results unless the parties have fully satisfied themselves about the effect of the legal system of their choice on any interpretation of their contract. In particular, in some jurisdictions, arbitrators have the right to adapt a contract to what they see as appropriate to the circumstances.[4]

It has been suggested[5] that in international joint ventures involving several parties there is a good case for multi-party arbitration. This would appear to have validity where all parties seek a resolution of the same problem and can thus minimize time and expense; but it must be borne in mind that many disputes, even in a multi-party international joint venture, may not be of that character.

---

4 See K. Zweigert and von Hoffmann, pp. 209 et seq.
5 J. Gilles Wetter, 'A multi-party arbitration scheme for international joint ventures', in *Arbitration International* (1987), pp. 2 et seq., refers to projects, i.e. contractual joint ventures.

Chapter 6

Legal Form

The choice of the appropriate legal form for operating a joint venture is of course governed by many other considerations. In both the US and the UK, formation of limited companies for limited and purely temporary purposes is relatively easy and not too costly in terms of administrative requirements and tax. Other legal systems, particularly in Continental Europe, can sometimes place greater obstacles in the way of the formation of such companies. There may be successive stages of taxation as money passes through to the participants and, in a company owned by two or three parties only, the liability for its debts might well spill over to its owners. They will also, in certain circumstances, have to suffer tax disadvantages if the operation is not profitable, but may be seen by the fiscal authorities to have been conducted for the benefit of the participants. In the countries in which this applies there is therefore in general a greater reluctance to enter into corporate joint ventures than under the Anglo-American systems.

Broadly a joint venture can be organized in one of three ways:

(a) a purely contractual joint venture;

(b) a partnership; or

(c) a limited liability company.

There are a number of variants on these themes, such as the limited liability partnership, and these are dealt with in more detail below.

Under English Law, each of the three basic structures is freely available. They could even be used in combination so that a partnership created by the joint venturers might choose to operate through a limited company. In the US, corporations used not to be able to enter into partnerships (see Baker and Cary, p. 368), but the laws of most states now permit a corporation to do so although a specific power may be required under the corporation's charter.

A. CONSORTIUM AGREEMENT WITHOUT CREATING LEGAL ENTITY

The situation in other countries, particularly Europe, is quite different.[1] Where for tax or other reasons operation through a limited liability company is undesirable, there is naturally an interest in bringing about the same situation as nearly as possible on a contractual basis. Particularly in France, where the parties contribute assets and intend to share the profits of an enterprise, the result, even though expressed as a contract, can very well be the establishment of a so-called *société de fait* which can bring about a result quite different from what the parties intended, involving unfortunate consequences, particularly in terms of tax and liability to third parties. Other European legal systems, particularly in Germany and Belgium, have suitable forms of association which appear to reduce the impact of these problems.[2]

On the other hand, profit-sharing is not necessarily an essential ingredient of a joint venture, at least not as a primary object. Parties which combine for the execution of a project in which each of the parties has its own area of supply and responsibility will normally intend to make any available profit in the 'parent' companies and will have laid down in detail how any penalties for default and other losses are to be shared out. Any profit in the joint venture then becomes only a residual item. It should be noted that while the definition of a joint venture postulates common control, this is not nullified by naming one of the parties as the spokesman (*chef de file*) in relation to outside parties. It is also conceivable that some of the joint venturers do not wish to appear publicly in that role and their participation is not disclosed; but for reasons explained later in this section, such an arrangement, though legally possible, is unlikely in cases in which a major contractual liability may be involved.

Clearly, a purely contractual structure will not normally be suitable for ventures of undefined duration. An important exception occurs in

---

1 For a detailed treatment, see Dubisson.
2 See Müller-Gugenberger and also Paillusseau and Lecerf, p. 139.

the case of the oil and gas industry where the practice of contractual cooperation through Joint Operating Agreements is well established. Under a Joint Operating Agreement, the parties agree to share the expenses and risks associated with the exploration and development of an oil field, but each party has the right to take its share of petroleum in kind and dispose of it separately in its own business. Amongst other things, this arrangement is designed to avoid the parties' relationship being treated as a partnership under English law, which would be the probable consequence of an agreement to share net profits.

Where the relationship is solely contractual, one of its principal aims will be to define the liabilities of the parties towards each other. These matters are dealt with in great detail by Mercadal and Janin, but that book also deals with many contractual matters which fall outside the definition of a joint venture adopted in this study.[3] In relation to contractual joint ventures in the mining and petroleum field, an Australian author[4] stresses the importance of default clauses, both as a disincentive against default and as a method by which the continuation of a joint venture can be assured in the event of default by one of the parties. To deal with the contractual problems vis-à-vis the third party would fall outside the scope of this book. Some of the problems of limitation of risk are dealt with by the original author and R. Hadley in *Contracting and Subcontracting for Overseas Projects*, pp. 11–12. It is perhaps sufficient to point out here that a purchaser of a large project, in seeking to contract with a group rather than a single party, is clearly, among other things, seeking to get the widest possible acceptance of responsibility for the project. If then that group interposes between itself and the purchaser a contracting unit in whatever legal form, the purchaser will wish to ensure that his security remains undiminished, whether by means of guarantees given by the participants in the venture or otherwise.

---

3 See also 'Accords de coopération inter-entreprises pour la réalisation de marchés internationaux', in 5 *Droit et Pratique du Commerce International* (1979), p. 337.

4 A. F. Mizen, 'Default by Joint Venturers', in *Australian Mining and Petrochemical Law Association Yearbook* (1985), pp. 91 et seq.

B. PARTNERSHIP

The possibility of the parties joining up in partnership to conduct a joint venture has been mentioned. In the Anglo-American systems, in which there is no difficulty in creating and operating limited liability companies, such partnerships are comparatively rare. They do, however, in certain circumstances, particularly where the joint venture is situated in the same country or countries as the participants, sometimes offer fiscal advantages, in that losses in the joint venture which could not be used to offset profits earned by the participants if the joint venture were a separate corporation, may be allowable to the partners in a partnership. It can therefore, in circumstances where the risk of unlimited joint liability is not a deterrent, be desirable to leave a joint venture in an unincorporated form during its initial phase and to incorporate it later when the risk of unrelieved losses has diminished.

Although a partnership cannot itself have limited liability, it is possible for those establishing the partnership to make their investment through an intermediate company specially formed for the purpose. The liability of the ultimate participant for the joint venture's debts is then limited to the assets of the special purpose company. Whilst this structure has its attractions, it should be noted that the ultimate participant may suffer adverse publicity if it allows its subsidiary, the special purpose company, to become insolvent. There could also be other undesired consequences, such as breaches of loan covenants or adverse effect on the parent's credit rating.

It is in any case important for the parties to consider precisely the form their arrangements are to take. They may otherwise be seen to have entered into a partnership even if they were not necessarily conscious of doing so.[5]

---

5 See, e.g. *Man v D'Arcy* [1968] 1 WLR 893, which deals with a case where one partnership by joining in a joint venture with another party becomes a partner in the partnership established by that joint venture. For a more general discussion of the role of partnership and unincorporated associations in English law, see Brown.

C. LIMITED LIABILITY COMPANY – ITS STATUS IN PARENTS' GROUP

Most long-term joint ventures are operated through a corporate entity. The precise legal form must vary from country to country, but in most jurisdictions there is no such thing as a joint venture company as such and an appropriate company is adapted by tailoring its constitutional documents to suit the needs of the situation.[6] In England it will normally be a (private) limited company but in exceptional cases a public limited company (plc) may be used, particularly if some of its financial needs are to be raised direct from the public.

In terms of Anglo-American accounting practice a proper joint venture will not normally be a subsidiary of any of its parent companies because they are sharing control. It will therefore be dealt with by the parent as an associated company and, in normal circumstances, be accounted for under the equity method or something akin to it. The accounting implications are dealt with in more detail in Chapter 11. There will, however, be some cases which in a business sense are joint ventures but where, due to the detailed arrangement of shareholdings and voting rights, the enterprise can be considered a subsidiary of one of the participants for the purposes of consolidation. This is sometimes brought about by giving one of the parties just over 50 per cent of the equity but still requiring the other party's consent to all major decisions as set out more fully on pp. 51–52. In certain circumstances participants may use the equity method as a way of withholding detailed information from their own shareholders, and this results in pressure to change the accounting treatment.[7]

Of course a joint venture may have one or more subsidiaries but the

---

6 In China, it was possible, until recently, for a joint venture to be formed under the Sino-Foreign Cooperative Joint Venture Law as either an unincorporated association (with unlimited liability), a limited liability company or a limited liability entity formed in accordance with Article 41 of the General Principles of the Law. Joint ventures within this third category had most of the characteristics of limited liability companies, but were not companies in the strict sense. It would appear that the option to form a 'hybrid' entity under Article 41 has now been removed by Article 14 of the Implementing Rules for the Cooperative Joint Venture Law. However, the distinction between cooperative joint ventures formed as unincorporated associations and those formed as limited liability companies remains.

7 See, e.g. Berg and Friedman, *Mergers and Acquisitions*, III (1979), p. 23.

joint venture itself may be conducted through more than one company, possibly in different countries, where in each case control is shared by the joint venturers. In some cases, participation is not divided equally so that one party has more than 50 per cent of the shares in joint venture company A and the other similarly more than 50 per cent in joint venture company B. One well-known case of this nature is the arrangement (long since abandoned) between the General Electric Company of the US and the French Compagnie des Machines Bull.[8]

As already indicated, it would be outside the scope of this book to examine country by country the precise legal form of such a corporation. In view of what was earlier said about the sharing of responsibility, attention should however, in general terms, be drawn to the fact that under some continental systems the liability of the owners for the debts of some types of corporation cannot be as clearly excluded, as is the case under the Anglo-American systems.

D. LIMITED PARTNERSHIPS

Where the participants wish to achieve tax transparency but are concerned to avoid the unlimited liability which would follow from setting up a partnership, the alternative of a limited partnership may be available.

Under a limited partnership, certain partners provide finance as passive or 'sleeping' partners without incurring unlimited liability, whilst the business of the partnership is managed by a general partner who need not make a capital contribution but must accept unlimited liability. An example of such an arrangement is International Private Satellite Partners, L.P., a Delaware limited partnership which owns and operates one of the first privately owned international satellite communications systems. The business of the limited partnership is managed by the general partner, Orion Satellite Corporation, a Delaware corporation which assumes unlimited liability for the partnership's obligations, but itself has limited liability under Delaware law. Under English law the Limited Partnerships Act 1907 imposes certain requirements on limited partnerships, which must be strictly observed, as

---

8 See Landon, pp. 238 et seq. For other examples, see Gullander, *Columbia Journal of World Business*, p. 111.

failure to do so may cause the partnership to lose its limited liability. The most important of these is that the limited partners must not become involved in the management of the partnership. Unfortunately, there is little authority as to what constitutes 'becoming involved in the management'. In a joint venture situation, where the parties generally wish to reserve certain important decisions to themselves, the uncertainty in this area is undesirable, and this is probably the reason why limited partnerships are not particularly common in the UK. Limited partnerships have proved more popular in the US, particularly as a medium for investment funds, where they enjoy certain fiscal advantages.

E. EUROPEAN ECONOMIC INTEREST GROUPING (EEIG)

With a view to encouraging cross-border alliances within the European Union, the European Commission has created a special vehicle for relatively small joint ventures between parties in different member countries, known as the European Economic Interest Grouping, or EEIG. The relevant Community legislation is contained in Council Regulation (EEC) No. 2137/85 which, whilst directly applicable in Member States, requires appropriate legislation to be passed under the domestic law of Member States for its implementation.

EEIGs have the following characteristics, some of which are rather unusual:

(1) there must be members from at least two different Member States of the European Union;

(2) the activities of the EEIG must be ancillary to those of its members;

(3) it cannot have more than 500 employees;

(4) no member may have a majority of votes;

(5) the members have unlimited joint and several liability for the EEIGs' debts.

An EEIG is formed by the parties entering into a formation contract, which is then registered at an official registry designated by domestic legislation (in the UK, this is Companies House). There are therefore limited publicity requirements. Whether the EEIG will have legal personality or not would appear to be determined by domestic legislation. From a taxation point of view, the acts of the EEIG are treated as those of its members, i.e. it is fiscally transparent.

Although the restrictions on what an EEIG can do, coupled with the unlimited liability of members, would suggest that EEIGs will have limited appeal, there have been a number of examples of EEIGs being formed between professional firms, such as solicitors and accountants, and trade associations. It may also prove to be a suitable vehicle for R&D collaboration between companies based in the European Union.

The European Commission has also proposed a draft European Company Statute for the creation of a European Company which could, if implemented, become a vehicle for cross-border joint ventures in the European Union. However, the progress of these proposals has for some time been blocked by the resistance in certain Member States to the associated requirement for employee participation in management of companies established under these arrangements. It is therefore too early to say whether and in what way this will have a role to play in future cross-border joint ventures.

Chapter 7

Agreements Between Parties Concerning the Proposed Joint Venture

This chapter provides a detailed description of the legal and organizational framework of a corporate joint venture.[1] In the simplest case, it is just conceivable that the rights of the parties can be adequately defined in the basic documents with which the company is formed, i.e. memorandum of association (in US, certificate of incorporation) and articles of association (by-laws). In some legal systems, this course is almost inevitable because agreements between shareholders about the conduct of a limited liability company are not enforceable.

In order to discuss fully the scope and intent of such agreements, it will be assumed that they are enforceable except to the extent to which they offend against specific legal prohibitions. In any case, such agreements may contain clauses which do not bear directly on the conduct of the joint venture company and thus are not likely to be unenforceable.

In addition to agreements among intended shareholders, there is often a need for agreements with the joint venture company. Drafts of such agreements will normally form an integral part of the agreement between future shareholders, and the participants will undertake to procure that the new company enters into these agreements before they commit significant funds to the joint venture.

Since the parties will normally be protected against changes in the company statutes, a Shareholders' Agreement may, in some circum-

---

1 Some of the topics may also require attention in certain contractual joint ventures.

stances, not need to survive the formation of the company and the execution of those basic agreements to which that company is a party. Sometimes the agreements between the participants are split up into more than one agreement, e.g. one defining the joint business objective and one or more others dealing with control and management of the jointly owned corporation. This may have particular merit when only part of the basic agreement is meant to survive incorporation and may also be useful in cases in which enforceability of one or other provision is in doubt.

As will be seen, there is a wide variety of topics and possible situations to cover; the more fully they are considered the less likely there will be future disagreements and unexpected risks (see Gavin).

One point is common to all such agreements: the importance of defining precisely the business of the proposed joint venture. This is particularly vital when one or more participants are already engaged in the kind of business for which the joint venture is planned – possibly in a wider field than that proposed for the joint venture – and can affect the competition aspects dealt with in Chapter 13. The parties are always free to redefine the business by a variation to their agreement if circumstances so require.

It should be noted that, in the absence of specific agreement at the time of the transfer, the provisions of a Shareholders' Agreement may not be binding on a transferee of shares in the joint venture company. Furthermore, an agreement between the shareholders of the company will not normally be binding on the company itself. These difficulties may be overcome by making the company a party to the Shareholders' Agreement, so that the provisions can be directly enforced against the company. However, this strategy needs to be treated with caution. A recent English case, *Russell v Northern Bank Development Corporation* [1992] 3 All ER 167,[2] appeared to confirm the principle, under English law, that any provision in a Shareholders' Agreement which is inconsistent with a statutory power of the company is ineffective and unenforceable against the company. Furthermore, if it is not possible to sever that provision from the rest of the agreement, the entire Shareholders'

---

2 The *Russell* case involved a restriction on the company's statutory power to increase its share capital. The case is not uncontroversial – see B. Davenport *What did 'Russell' decide?* BJIBFL Vol. 8 No. 10 p. 469.

Agreement may be invalid. Similar difficulties are thought to arise under the laws of some other jurisdictions.

A. BASIC SHAREHOLDERS' AGREEMENT

The possible contents of the Shareholders' Agreement can be divided between certain basic elements which are always either present or deliberately omitted and which require attention regardless of the precise nature of the joint venture, and a rather larger variety of topics which are more dependent on the precise circumstances and of which any list cannot therefore be considered exhaustive. In addition to a precise definition of the purpose and scope of the joint venture, the following fall into the former category.

(1) Funding requirements and the organization of the capital structure of the company.

(2) The relationship between the parties, including: (i) transferability of shares; (ii) minority protection; and (iii) provision for deadlock.

(3) Discontinuance of the corporation for reasons other than deadlock.

(4) Composition of board and management.

(5) Any restrictions on competition between the parties and the joint venture or between each other.

Funding Requirements and the Organization of the Capital Structure of the Company

The parties will normally agree to provide funds to the joint venture in accordance with their respective interests, either in the form of share capital or debt finance, or a mixture of the two. Any debt finance may come either from the parties themselves or from external sources (e.g. banks), in which case shareholder guarantees may well be required. The choice of funding method will depend on a number of factors, including some, or all, of the following:

— Generally speaking, loan finance will be more flexible than share capital in that repayment of a loan is likely to be quite straightforward, whilst reduction in share capital will only be permitted if the relevant statutory conditions and procedures have been complied with.

— In certain jurisdictions (although not currently in the UK), there may be taxes or duties on the amount of share capital subscribed, whereas loan finance would be free of such taxes.

— It may be possible for the joint venture to deduct interest paid under shareholder loans in calculating taxable profits, whilst dividend payments are not generally tax deductible. This could mean that shareholder loans receive more favourable tax treatment than equity. However, 'thin capitalisation' rules in many jurisdictions may result in interest being treated for tax purposes as if it were a dividend payment where loan finance exceeds a certain ratio to equity finance.

— It will frequently be advantageous to locate debt finance in the jurisdiction with the highest tax rates, so as to obtain maximum tax relief for the interest payments. Thus, where the joint venture is to be established in a country with high tax rates it will usually be sensible for the participants to fund the joint venture by means of loan finance. Where, on the other hand, tax rates are higher in a participant's home jurisdiction, it would, subject to other factors being equal, be preferable for that participant to borrow funds in its own jurisdiction and subscribe for equity.

— The participants may wish to demonstrate the worth of the joint venture to third parties, such as landlords, banks or trading partners. In this case, a certain level of share capital will be required.

The structure of a joint venture company's share capital can be as simple or as complex as the circumstances require. In a straightforward situation the parties will simply subscribe for ordinary shares. A refinement of this is to create different classes of shares (normally described as 'A' Shares, 'B' Shares, etc.) with generally equal rights such as the right to appoint one or more directors, to attend meetings or to vote on certain issues, but otherwise ranking for dividends and capital as if they were ordinary shares. Among other things, this is a useful way of giving each party control over the appointment and withdrawal of directors under legal systems which do not permit directors to be nominated by a party.

Sometimes, more complex capital structures are employed, particularly where there are outside investors who are not involved in the management of the joint venture, as is the case in management buy-outs.

The consideration for shares subscribed by the participants may be cash but, in many instances, one or more of the parties will receive shares for non-cash consideration such as the transfer or grant of industrial property rights or the transfer of land, plant and machinery or other tangible assets. This topic is dealt with in more detail on pp. 59–60 below.

Rights of the Parties

(i) *Transferability of shares*

Parties entering into a joint venture do not normally expect the right to dispose freely of their shareholdings; nor do they consider the other party free to dispose of its holdings because the result could well be that two totally incompatible parties are thrown together. It is therefore usual for joint ventures to adopt a legal form where the transfer of shares can either be forbidden outright indefinitely (which is not generally acceptable in the US) or for a stated period, or where at any rate it is subject to board approval.

An alternative is not to restrict the transferability of the shares but to give the other shareholders a pre-emption right. This raises a difficulty concerning price arising from the fact that by the very nature of a joint venture, the shareholdings in it have no established market value. The possible choices appear to lie between the right to match a bona fide offer from outside and a pre-emption right based on a valuation by a third party expert. If the parties opt for a third party valuation, it is usual to set out the mechanism for appointing the expert and the basis of valuation in some detail in the Shareholders' Agreement. It should be borne in mind that many of the assumptions referred to in provisions of this type are likely to be hypothetical as there will seldom be a ready market for the joint venture company's shares. In view of the nature of a joint venture, it is common that whatever rules govern the transferability of the shares allow only disposal of a party's entire holding.

The Shareholders' Agreement will sometimes include a 'bring along' clause. This is a provision which requires that a participant wishing to transfer its shares to a third party must attempt to procure that the notice given to the other participants under the pre-emption clause must be accompanied by an offer from the third party to the continuing participants to buy out their shares on the same terms as those set out in the notice. Appendix III E contains an example of such a clause.

It is common to make an exception to the pre-emption clause for a transfer to another company within the same group as the original shareholder. This should always be subject to the proviso that the shares must be transferred back to the original participant if the transferee company is subsequently sold to a company outside the group. Failure to provide for this will enable a party so minded to override the pre-emption provisions 'by the back door'.

Where an interest is transferred to a third party, it may be desirable to require the incoming party to enter into an undertaking to be bound by the provisions of the Shareholders' Agreement. This document, which is commonly referred to in the UK as a 'Deed of Adherence', also provides a convenient mechanism for releasing a departing shareholder from its obligations.

No share transfer is of course involved where one of the participants is acquired by someone else, but, by changing ultimate control, this can bring about a totally unintended situation in which one party finds itself in a joint venture with a party it did not intend to collaborate with. To guard against such a possibility, it may be desirable to give the other party certain rights of pre-emption of the acquired party's holding or of disposal of its own holding, possibly in a manner somewhat analogous to that sometimes chosen for deadlock situations (see p. 54 below). That may render a participant whose interest in the joint venture represents a substantial part of his assets less vulnerable to hostile bids from outsiders. Another case for advance regulation is the insolvency of a participant.

How virtually impossible it is to deal with all possible situations in advance in a totally unambiguous manner is perhaps best demonstrated by the court proceedings[3] concerning GEC's 50 per cent holding in GPT, a joint venture with the Plessey Company, which was itself the subject of a bid by a joint venture in which GEC is a participant.

Clearly, one important reason why transfers of shares are restricted is

---

3 *The Plessey Company plc v The General Electric Company plc and others*: Ch. Div. (Mr Justice Morritt) 14 February 1989; Court of Appeal (LJs Kerr, Nourse and Staughton) 22 March 1989. Although all the judges reached the same conclusion, they arrived at it with considerable divergence in detail, and lawyers drafting similar agreements in future will find that careful study of these judgments may help to obviate similar litigation.

the fact that, more often than not, the selling participant will be in a continuing contractual relationship with the joint venture and, possibly, also with the other participants. It is not sufficient to agree that these agreements must be transferred to the new shareholder because certain obligations, such as confidentiality, have to be continued by the original shareholder and for some of the others the new shareholder may not be a suitable party. Termination of the agreements is dealt with in Chapter 9. Similar considerations will apply on discontinuance of a joint venture.

When an additional party is to become a member of the joint venture, this is normally achieved by letting the new party subscribe for new shares or by transferring shares from existing participants, or by a mixture of both. In most cases it is not practicable to deal with this situation fully in the initial agreements and a renegotiation is required. There are exceptions to this rule; when, say, three parties wish to create a joint venture but one of them is temporarily unable to join, its rights and obligations on joining may well be spelled out in advance.

(ii) Minority protection

Where the shareholdings of the parties are unequal, and where more than two parties are involved, minority protection forms an important matter for agreement. The simplest way of achieving it is to require unanimity (or a suitably qualified majority) for resolutions at share-holders' and directors' meetings and to define the quorum for meetings in such a way as to ensure avoidance of snap decisions. Even this may not be enough without a definition of the topics requiring a positive resolution by directors or shareholders, so that management, which may well be associated with one or other party, cannot without approval do those things which, if resolved by the board or the shareholders, would require unanimity. In the following pages unanimity and qualified majority are treated interchangeably. A comprehensive list of items requiring unanimity is set out in Appendix III.

Where it is known or envisaged that the joint venture corporation will itself have subsidiaries, then the Shareholders' Agreement will, where it is permissible, be a convenient place to extend these limitations to subsidiaries. Since the subsidiary of a joint venture corporation will not itself have the participants as shareholders, these limitations on its freedom can only be brought about indirectly by preventing the parent company from prompting certain actions in subsidiaries without the requisite shareholders' or board approval in the parent. An alternative may be not to set up such offshoots as subsidiaries of the joint venture but as parallel joint ventures, but this may often have tax and other disadvantages.

In some cases, the list of items for joint approval may, due to the nature of the business and the relationship of the parties, include many more items which would normally be left to management, such as patent and trademark applications and the grant of licences and franchises, as well as sensitive matters such as dealings with participants. In addition, of course, any changes in the company's statutes (articles of association, by-laws) will usually require unanimity.

On the other hand, there are certain items where a unanimity requirement may produce an unintended result. An obvious case of this nature is the distribution of available profit, to which one party to a joint venture may attach greater importance than the other. One method of overcoming this problem is, where two parties to a joint venture have separate classes of shares, to invest them with separate dividend rights so that, within certain pre-agreed limits, one party can declare a dividend regardless of co-operation by the other. See p. 62 and Appendix III D.

In cases where the joint venture is a vehicle for handling contracts to which the participants make a major contribution by way of sub-contracts many further matters may need spelling out in the basic agreements.

(iii) Deadlock

Evidently, the more matters are required to be dealt with on the basis of unanimity, the greater is the risk that the venture will experience a conflict which cannot be resolved and which, if serious enough, will produce deadlock. The very threat this poses to the continued well-being of the venture can act as a strong deterrent for either party to bring this situation about. On the other hand, if one of the joint venturers sees an advantage in bringing about a deadlock situation, it is normally not difficult for him to create one. Some Shareholders' Agreements provide for periodic review of the agreement for the purpose of avoiding outright deadlock, and also of ensuring that the contractual relationships between the parties remain suitable to the tasks in hand.

When dealing with deadlock, distinction is sometimes made between legal disputes and management disputes. Legal disputes are those which concern the interpretation of the parties' rights and obligations under the Shareholders' Agreement and are normally best submitted to the court to decide or referred to arbitration. Management disputes, on the other hand, concern issues such as the policy or direction of the joint venture and are not necessarily capable of resolution through legal proceedings. Attempts must normally be made to resolve them by some other means.

In the event of deadlock, under some legal systems (e.g. English law) either party may ask the court to dissolve the company (see *A & BC Chewing Gum Ltd* [1975] 1 All ER 1017).[4] In addition there are a number of alternatives available to the parties which can make provision in the Shareholders' Agreement for this eventuality. A casting vote (e.g. for the chairman) will avoid deadlock but will do so by giving the party whose nominee he is an advantage overriding the concept of common control. Another method which has been tried is to submit the dispute to binding arbitration but, apart from the fact that an arbitrator or a body of arbitrators would not readily have sufficient knowledge of the business in question to enable him or them to arrive with some certainty at a reasonable solution, an aggrieved party may very well provoke another deadlock before long, all of which can only act to the detriment of the joint venture. A similar approach is to provide an additional independent outside director (a so-called 'swingman' director) for the express purpose of resolving board deadlock[5] or a small shareholder with a balancing vote[6] but the objections are similar to those relating to an arbitrator. The same doubts must apply to the appointment of a third person under ICC Rules (Adaptation of Contracts, Publication No. 326 refers specifically to joint venture management disputes). In the US the corporation laws of many states authorize the court to appoint a director where a corporation is deadlocked. For that reason, it is common practice to have a swingman director where board seats are equally divided between the parties in order to ensure that the more drastic remedy of petitioning the court to appoint a director never arises. A somewhat more satisfactory option can be to provide for the disagreement to be referred for resolution to the chairmen or managing directors

---

4 In that case, the court held that the repudiation by one of the parties of the other's fundamental right to appoint a director was sufficient ground to enable the court to order the winding up of the company under the principle established in *Ebrahami* v *Westbourne Galleries* [1972] 2 All ER 492.

5 See, e.g. *Harvard Law Review* (1964/5), pp. 408 et seq.

6 See Gullander, *Columbia Journal of World Business*, p. 110 and the AEG–Mostek deal as reported in *The Financial Times* (1982), 4 June, in which a bank was envisaged in that role.

of the shareholders in the hope that they may be able to stand back from the issues and take a more reasonable view than those directly involved in the joint venture. This still leaves open the possibility that those entrusted with resolving the dispute may be unable to reach agreement, in which case, one of the options described in the following paragraph may be appropriate.

In the absence of a compromise via one or other of the above methods, the remedies commonly used are aimed at liquidation of the joint venture or transferring outright ownership to one or other party. One formula which has been used quite frequently is for party A to have the right to put its shares to party B at a price of its own choice. Party B must then either accept or reverse the process by putting its shareholding to party A at the identical price. This mechanism is frequently referred to as 'Texas shootout' or 'Russian roulette'. The risk of reversal acts, of course, against the choice of an unreasonable price. There are a number of variations on this theme, but their effect is broadly similar. These methods of resolving deadlocks, if there are no other restrictions such as restraint on foreign ownership, work reasonably well if the parties' shareholdings are roughly equal and the parties themselves are of not too disparate strength.[7] Difficulties may well arise where the technology on which the business is based is provided substantially by one party only or where one of the parties does not have sufficient resources to buy out the other. For all these reasons parties often choose not to legislate against deadlock but to rely on the restraint induced by the very threat of deadlock. As stated, joint venturers often stipulate a periodic review of their agreements but, while this can help in overcoming problems not foreseen at the outset, it cannot overcome a deep-seated deadlock situation.

Deadlock may arise less frequently when there are more than two parties but because of the minority protection discussed above it is still an obvious possibility. Its resolution through a form of buy-out arrangement may, on the other hand, be more difficult; the 'minority' party may well have substantially more than 50 per cent of the total to acquire and, in the opposite case, matters would have to be so arranged that the remaining partners have proportionate rights and the situation

---

7 Segall and Sirkin give, as an example of what they term 'executive joint ventures', one in which an executive who is meant to run the business is given an equity participation. This term does not appear to have gained general acceptance.

has to be covered in which not all the remaining parties wish to join in taking over the 'minority' party's stake.

In international joint ventures involving countries with restrictions on inward investment, provisions for future buy-out of a participant will be unenforceable. It will hardly be possible to get the necessary approval in advance at the time when the joint venture is entered into, and risky to rely on getting it when needed and having it implemented. Thus, the only remedy available to the foreign party is a put option enabling him to require the local party(s) to buy his shares. This may be of limited value where there are doubts as to the creditworthiness of the local party(s) or where exchange control restrictions would prevent the foreign party from repatriating the proceeds of sale.

In cases in which the dissolution of a joint venture does not arise out of provisions in the original agreement but is decided by the parties at a later stage, there will often have to be a special termination agreement which is discussed on p. 74.

Discontinuance (other than Deadlock)

Company laws in advanced legal systems normally deal in considerable detail with the dissolution of a corporation. This section only considers matters concerning the dissolution which need to be spelled out in the Shareholders' Agreement. There may be a minimum period during the initial life of a joint venture in which one or both parties would wish to avoid dissolution. This is normally equal to the period necessary to enable the joint venture to achieve its initial objectives and, where appropriate, repay any loan finance. Providing it is not forced on the corporation by insolvency, joint control over the corporation would normally suffice to ensure this object, though it must be recognized that it would be extremely difficult to carry on a joint venture if one party were determined to bring it to an end.

Where a joint venture company has lost its capital and there is an asset deficiency, under normal rules the unsecured creditors suffer rateably. Participants may be anxious to avoid such a situation for protection of their own name and credit standing and be willing to bail out the joint venture, as they might in similar circumstances do with a subsidiary. They would, of course, expect their co-venturers to participate in making up the deficiency. Since neither party would be anxious to write what amounts to an open cheque, it may be difficult to find a satisfactory formula by which such occurrences can be provided for in the shareholders' agreement. One possible solution is to provide for termination and subsequent liquidation of the joint venture company if there is an asset deficiency which is not, within a short period, made good by subscription of further capital. However, it must also be recognized that when parties are negotiating a joint venture, it may be psychologically difficult to spell out the results of failure in great detail and to negotiate on them. The question of additional financing requirements is dealt with on p. 61. Since there are likely to be agreements between the participants and between one or more of them and the joint venture corporation, the effects of discontinuance on them will require careful examination. (See also Chapter 9.)

Composition of Board and Management

In legal systems in which shareholders can have the right to nominate directors, it may be sufficient to lay down the number of each party's directors. As a matter of goodwill such nominations are often made subject to consultation or even approval by the other party. Where directors have to be elected, the safest way of ensuring a given number to any party is the provision of separate classes of shares for the different participants, but this may not be possible under the company laws of many jurisdictions. In any case, the principal matters for attention are the quorum and the requirements of either unanimity or qualified majorities. If there is to be a board chairman, this is often arranged on a rotating basis. It is not usual to give the chairman a casting vote which could easily upset the carefully contrived balance of voting arrangements (see p. 48) and might turn the joint venture company into a subsidiary of the participant who controls the casting vote.

It is important to remember in this connection that directors, whether elected or non-elected, have a duty to the company of which they are directors which is stronger than their duty to those who appoint them. In this connection, Broden and Scanlon discuss the validity of voting agreements made between some, but not all, of the participants. In general they approve of such arrangements under American law but it should be assumed that when the directors' duty to the joint venture corporation comes into conflict with such arrangements, it takes precedence. This is frequently a reason for stipulating that some or all of the reserved matters are to be referred to the shareholders rather than the board.

The parties will wish to lay down in advance how the corporation is to be managed and make provision for the appointment of the chief executive and possibly some of his senior staff. Since he is meant to manage the company for the benefit of all participants, it is not generally desirable for him to have a vote at board meetings and, for this reason, the chief executive is usually not a member of the board. This of course presents no problem in legal systems in which the board of management is separate from the supervisory board.

In regard to the management of a joint venture, as distinct from its direction, a useful distinction has been drawn between a coalition type management made up of nominees of the parties and an autonomous management which runs the joint venture as an independent enterprise and only has to turn to its board, representing the participants, on major decisions (see Kolde, *The Multinational Company*). Sometimes one of the participants is appointed as managing partner for the enterprise under a separate management agreement. In this situation, the other parties will wish to ensure that the managing party is required to refer back to them for major decisions, otherwise they could find that their rights under the shareholders' agreement are eroded by the management agreement. In practical terms in the early stages a coalition type of management may be unavoidable even where greater autonomy is the ultimate goal.

It has been rightly suggested[8] that one party often dominates a joint venture (by its own size, or by the size of its equity interest, etc.) but where there is such a disparity, possibly in the size of the participants, it is doubly important that the management structure should be carefully laid down in advance.

Competition by and with Participants

This is a problem which must by definition affect every joint venture, whether it is specifically dealt with in agreements or not.[9] Since competitive activity is a matter of future conduct during the life of a joint venture it may arise even when at the outset neither party engages in the proposed activity of the joint venture. It can come about as a side effect of an otherwise unrelated transaction, for instance an acquisition by one of the parties which, perhaps in only a minor way, includes an activity which is in competition with the joint venture.

---

8 E.g. by J. P. Killing who speaks of a 'dominant partner'.
9 For an example of a detailed definition of the competitive rights of parties in a publishing venture, see *Hachette S.A. and Langenscheidt KG* [1982] 1 CMLR 181.

This is equally a problem for contractual joint ventures. When parties enter into a joint tendering arrangement, they will normally have to undertake not to bid for the same project on their own or in association with others. This undertaking may be qualified in many ways, particularly as regards time. In addition, there may be freedom to act as a subcontractor to another party as well as other limitations of the undertakings given.

As regards corporate joint ventures, the question of competition arises both in regard to the rights of the participants and in regard to those of the joint venture. Where one party is already engaged in the type of business into which the joint venture is entering and the joint venture represents a territorial extension, it must be implied that the shareholder will not compete with the joint venture in its territory. This may be satisfactory at the outset but to what extent such an undertaking remains enforceable over an indefinite period of time, must certainly be open to doubt. Moreover, a joint venture in the course of normal development may well turn into a business not clearly encompassed by its original definition.

Particularly in such a case, the participant already engaged in its proposed activity will wish to limit the rights of the joint venture to operate to the territory for which it is being created. Where the joint venture is dependent on intellectual property rights licensed by the parent, this may provide adequate protection but, due to the impact of competition law on such arrangements, the validity of such a deal may well be questionable. Normally, joint managerial controls in practice suffice to ensure that the joint venture does not operate outside the limits and objects for which it was created. In any case, it must be borne in mind that the anti-monopoly authorities will concern themselves closely with the nature and scope of the proposed operation and wish to see limits both as to geographical area and duration on the restrictions which the parties may seek to impose. Also, particularly where a joint venture is set up in a less developed country to manufacture a product developed elsewhere, the authorities in the host country in many cases insist on defining export rights at least to certain areas before the transaction is approved as a whole. The foreign participants will then seek, as far as possible, to ensure marketing rights for themselves covering the joint venture's export to enable them to supervise proper adherence to these arrangements.

As already mentioned, it is important to recognize that future competition between a participant and the joint venture may come about in unintended ways, particularly where the participants are themselves large businesses. Such a company may acquire a business which has an ancillary activity that is competitive to the activities of the joint venture. A participant may thus find himself in an unintended breach of a non-competition undertaking, but even in the absence of such an undertaking the new acquisition may still be an irritant to the business of the joint venture.

Joint venture agreements often deal with the possibility of such a development. A solution may be found in compelling the acquirer to offer to sell the competitive business to the joint venture on terms defined in the agreement and to leave him free to operate it if the joint venture does not acquire it within a specified period, an action which the 'offending' participant must not frustrate. It will of course be understood that some of the governmental restrictions dealt with in Part IV of this book may make such a solution impossible to enforce fully.

B. SELECTIVE TOPICS FOR SHAREHOLDERS' AGREEMENT

Whereas the matters in the preceding section are topics for consideration in every joint venture, the ones which follow are only for consideration if in the particular joint venture under negotiation there is a reasonable chance that they may become problem areas. It may not be bad advice in all cases to consider all the items set out in the check-list in Appendix I on pp. 105–112 and, e.g. confidentiality undertakings might well have been included under A above. It will be appreciated on the other hand that particularly in dealing with governments or their institutions as a party to a joint venture it may not be practicable to negotiate many of these matters in advance, as would otherwise be desirable.

Transfer to the Joint Venture of One or More Existing Businesses

A party may already have an activity in the intended field of application of the joint venture, e.g. a branch or subsidiary, in its intended territory. In other cases, two parties may seek to merge not their entire businesses but their businesses in a specific field. In either case it is usually desirable for the one or more parties to receive an equity participation in the joint venture in return for the business assets brought in. Such an arrangement will require some form of valuation of the assets brought in which, under some legal systems, will require certification by an outside valuer to show that the shares have been issued for full consideration. In principle, the method of arriving at a proper value must not be different from that applicable to the sale of a business to a third party. This is equally true when all participants in a joint venture bring in business assets and, subject to particular circumstances, the basis of valuation must be equally applicable to all. Similarly, it will normally be appropriate for the party transferring the assets to the joint venture to give warranties and indemnities to the joint venture and/or the other party (parties) as in respect of any other business sale. A due diligence investigation may also be appropriate to verify the value of the assets being transferred and check for undisclosed liabilities.

In international joint ventures it is important to define the currencies in which the valuation is carried out. In a period of considerable instability of rates of exchange between major currencies, this can easily become a source of major disagreement. The participants may also have to make provision to protect a party against later devaluation, particularly when a government is involved in the joint venture.[10]

Often the value of assets transferred can only be finally ascertained after the effective date of the transfer. Also the shareholdings in the proposed venture may not depend exclusively on the value of the assets brought in, since relative earning power and other circumstances may well influence the size of the relative holdings. Where the value is not ascertainable in advance, the shareholdings of the parties may have to be based on estimated figures and a cash adjustment may be required to compensate for any valuation differences. Where the valuation turns out to exceed the estimate and a cash refund is impractical or undesirable, it may be necessary for the other party to adjust its contribution to bring about the desired result in terms of relative shareholdings.

The term 'assets' is used here to mean 'net assets', i.e. after deducting applicable liabilities, but this depends entirely on the arrangements of the parties. It must be understood that assets may include intangible items, such as business goodwill, access to technology and patents, and similar matters which will normally give rise to a 'goodwill' item in the opening balance sheet of the joint venture. This, in turn, may produce, under the accounting standards applicable in many of the principal countries today, a requirement for this item to be written off either

10 See, e.g. Ehinger, pp. 195–196.

immediately or by depreciation over a number of years. This of course will affect the joint venture's prospective fiscal position as well as the size of the distributable profit. In some instances, rather than forming a new company, the parties may wish to use a company already in existence and in the ownership of one of them. It may already be engaged in its future business activity but this is not necessarily so. In all such cases, the party contributing the corporation will have to indemnify other participants against unknown liabilities or other impediments to future trading.

It is common to provide that failure to complete the transfer by the agreed date will require the defaulting party to pay compensation to the other parties and/or the joint venture and a prolonged failure to do so will entitle the innocent parties to terminate the transaction.

Provision of Further Finance

A joint venture for the execution of a single contract or a joint research project may have its financial needs clearly established in advance. Even then, changes in the requirements occur frequently. In a business venture of indefinite duration, the participants may well hold widely differing views as to how future financial needs are to be met.

In a profitable venture it may be possible to accommodate future financial needs to some extent under the profit distribution policy that is adopted. Beyond that it would be desirable for the parties to lay down, at least for a number of years, by what method future finance should be raised, i.e. equity and/or borrowing, and to agree with each other limits up to which they are willing to provide future finance and the conditions (e.g. a call by management) with which they are bound in advance to comply. Where further equity capital is to be provided it is common for the Shareholders' Agreement and/or constitutional documents to pro-vide for such further equity to be offered pro rata to the existing participants in the first instance in order to preserve the balance of the participants' interests. Indeed, under most legal systems this would be the position anyway in the absence of agreement to the contrary. As far as the choice between equity and loan capital is concerned, most of the considerations referred to earlier in this chapter in the context of initial funding requirements will apply equally to future finance. It should be borne in mind that, particularly in countries which operate exchange control, any commitments to provide future finance may have to be made subject to any necessary government approvals. The parties may also wish to qualify their undertakings to avoid situations in which such calls are used to pay for losses incurred rather than for future expansion.

Despite all agreements and safeguards, a joint venture may well find itself with a financial need not envisaged in the original arrangements. Failing agreement between the participants, one party may be willing to put up the further finance or to accept an additional party to the venture. The results of such a situation can be legislated for in an agreement, for instance by providing that a party subscribing further capital unilaterally after the other has declined to participate acquires a correspondingly larger part of the equity. If this process carries too far, it may lead to a situation in which the minority partner has control rights out of proportion to his share in the investment. It may be possible to agree in advance that if one party's participation gets reduced beyond a certain point, it should have the right to sell its shares to the others, or the others should be entitled to buy it out. Alternatively, it might be agreed that the dividend rights of the party who has declined to put up additional equity should be temporarily suspended or that the party which is prepared to do so should receive a new class of share with a preferential rate of return. There are many possibilities. It will, however, be understood that it is virtually impossible to cater in advance for all such changes which may occur over a period of many years.

Distribution of Profit and Repatriation of Funds

Normally, in the absence of an effective majority, no one party can ensure that available profits are distributed as dividend. This may deprive it of an important means of control over a capital hungry joint venture. In such a case, the separate classes of shares given to the joint venturers (see p. 48 above) can provide a solution by giving the holder of either class of share a defined right to declare a dividend on his shares, which the other may match if it chooses to do so. In other cases the shareholders' agreement may lay down a fixed percentage of distributable profit to be paid as dividend so that a participant who voted against the appropriate resolution would be in breach of the shareholders' agreement.

In international joint ventures it is of course important to ensure, as far as possible, that funds due to a non-resident participant can be remitted to that party in the appropriate currency and to protect that party against devaluation of the local currency (see also p. 60).

Put and Call Options

When embarking on a joint venture, it is generally advisable for a participant to establish an exit route, whether to enable the participant to realize its investment at the end of the joint venture term or to extricate itself if things go wrong. One means of achieving this is through the use of options – for instance, Party A might have an option to require Party B to buy its shares (a 'put' option) or to buy Party B's shares (a 'call' option) by reference to a pre-agreed formula at certain specified times in the future or on the happening of certain events (e.g. the insolvency of Party B or a breach by Party B of some material provision of the Shareholders' Agreement). There are many possible variants. For instance, the basis of valuation may be more favourable to the 'innocent' party if the option is being exercised for a default-related reason. Alternatively, the parties might agree put and call options (see Appendix III) in the expectation that the joint venture will be transferred to one of the parties at the end of its term. It should be noted that the existence of options can have a significant impact on the tax status of the joint venture (see p. 85).

Trade with Participants

Some joint ventures can be regarded as virtually independent of the resources, other than financial, available from the participants, but others, probably in the great majority, are totally dependent on these resources. The joint venture may start life in premises of one of its parents at favourable rental terms and could be in severe difficulties if it lost not only the favourable rental but perhaps also the backing of common services which are more economical when shared with the parent. A joint venture, particularly one set up in a different country from the parent whose product it seeks to promote, may depend on the granting of industrial property rights, but more particularly on continuing availability of supplies at an acceptable price level. Also the provision of management and other services may form an integral part of the deal.

The normal way to deal with these matters in an organizational sense is to agree in advance on one or a series of contracts to be entered into between one or more of the participants and the joint venture and to arrange matters in such a way that they cannot be altered without the consent of the joint venturers. These agreements will then be recited in the Shareholders' Agreement and will form an essential part of the joint venture arrangements. It is of course possible, and quite normal, to build into such arrangements an amending formula under which the charges for goods and for other services, such as the loan of staff, are automatically adjusted from time to time.

Intellectual property rights can normally be made available for long periods of time. On the other hand, the parties will be hesitant to commit themselves to the supply of goods and services over a long period. The parent will wish its freedom to discontinue a product range not to be unduly restricted by an obligation to supply sets of parts to a foreign joint venture, possibly in quantities which would be uneconomical to manufacture or procure on their own. It is not really possible here to do more than highlight the problem, the solution to which must vary from case to case. It should, however, be emphasized that pricing policy between a parent and a joint venture, if it appears to favour one at the expense of the other, may become the concern of both customs and tax authorities in either country because these transactions are not regarded as arm's length arrangements and any authority which feels it is being deprived either of corporation tax or of customs duties will seek to rectify the situation. These authorities in any one country will often have opposing objectives. In addition, competitors may complain of dumping.

Parent Guarantees

Perhaps the most obvious case where parent guarantees are often demanded is that of a corporation formed to execute a large contract, often with a share capital relatively insignificant in relation to the contract value and its attendant risks. This is why parent guarantees may well be asked for by the other party to the contract and by lenders to whom the joint venture alone cannot offer adequate security or where at least, taken on its own, it would rate less favourable terms of borrowing.

A parent will normally, in such a case, wish to limit its guarantee to its proportionate interest but certainly there will be circumstances in which the parents are required each to guarantee the full amount and then to rely either on the Shareholders' Agreement or on an *ad hoc* arrangement to share the liability appropriately.

Management of the Joint Venture

As already indicated, there may be a great variety of other topics which require covering in such an agreement in a given case. It may be desirable

to lay down management routines, reporting arrangements, the provision of certain special services, and many other matters. These apply
particularly to a joint venture between an established manufacturer and
a governmental or government-sponsored organization in a less industrialized country. For the successful functioning of the venture it may be
necessary to second to the joint venture a certain number of people
working for the established manufacturer, but this undertaking cannot
be effective if the necessary work-permits and other administrative help
are not available at the right time and if such matters as the responsibility
for tax on seconded employees' earnings and the availability of
exit-permits for them are not adequately covered. There may also have to
be specific undertakings in regard to the repatriation of funds. It would
not be practicable to deal with these matters here in an exhaustive way,
and they are not specific to joint ventures. Information on the kinds of
safeguards required is available from studies which look at the problems
on a country by country basis, but it must be remembered that regulation
of such matters, particularly by government, tends to change frequently
and at short notice, and literature relating to many of the countries in
question may be out of date. Also, undertakings in these matters given by
governments may not be readily enforceable, particularly after a change
of political control in the country concerned. However, it may be
possible to cover the risk of breach of such undertakings under
investment insurance with an export credit agency or in the private
market.

Confidentiality Undertakings

As a result of common control over a joint venture, either party is liable
to obtain confidential information relating to the other. A mutual
confidentiality undertaking relating not only to the joint venture but also
to information concerning the participants, is therefore often included in
such agreements. Similarly, as a result of the collaboration in a joint
venture, each party's personnel is more exposed than usual to possible
poaching by the other party. In practice, this may put one of the parties in
a very much stronger position than the other – which is then likely to
seek contractual protection, though it must be recognized that such
undertakings are hard to enforce.

Chapter 8

Separate Agreements with Joint Venture

Joint ventures are in many cases dependent on contractual relationships with the participants which are likely to have been settled in advance within the framework of the joint venture agreement but which, to become binding for and against a joint venture corporation, must, after its incorporation, be formally entered into with the corporation itself. In cases where existing businesses are transferred to the joint venture or merged to come together in such a joint venture, such agreements may already be in existence and be transferred with the business. However, they may lack the necessary precision which may have been adequate for the relationship between a parent and a wholly owned subsidiary but will no longer be appropriate to the relationship of participants with a joint venture. Where in business terms the participants stand in a parallel relationship to the joint venture, it will normally be necessary to ensure that, as nearly as possible, the agreements with different participants are identical. It should, however, be stated that where the participants are domiciled in different countries, the need to comply with different laws may well mean that in practice the parties have to accept certain variations.

In industrial joint ventures the subjects to be covered by these agreements can be generally brought under the following three main headings.

A. Supply (both ways).
B. Services.
C. Intellectual property rights.

In the latter case, there are sometimes circumstances in which there is need for contingent agreements between the participants. Since such agreements are entirely dominated by the relevant agreements with the joint venture, it seems practical to discuss them in the present context.

A. SUPPLY

The need for agreements arises according to circumstances in two distinct ways. If the joint venture is intended to market, in a given territory, products of one of the joint venturers then it must be given the appropriate distribution rights, and the terms on which it obtains supply must be clearly spelled out as regards price, quality, consequences of failure to supply, etc. Often one of the greatest difficulties in this context is to agree a pattern which will be suitable for many years ahead.

Supply must be dealt with similarly in reverse circumstances. Where two parties join together for the production of a kind of material of which both have equal need – the joint venture being economically viable by enabling the required capital outlay to be justified and by allowing the parties together to enjoy an economy of scale which they could not obtain separately – then the joint venture is dependent on both parties sharing adequate utilization of its plant and, if necessary, suffering financial penalties for failure to utilize it in the intended manner. Such an agreement also will have to be valid for a considerable period to enable the investment to be amortized.

In some cases the joint venturer who already produces the product may accept a contract to buy a certain amount of the joint venture's output but the most important cases of this nature are joint mining enterprises which have developed a particular form of contract known as 'take or pay' agreements.

The reverse situation may also arise in which the joint venture cannot, at least temporarily, meet the full requirement of the joint venturers. This may come about either by production failures or as a result of demand which is larger than was anticipated. In practice, it will often arise through one or more parties being late in making its (or their) requirements known or specifying requirements which involve a degree of additional preparation. It is generally advisable to deal with these matters as fully as possible in the supply agreements, both as regards pricing and as regards priority of supply, but the short list of possibilities given above will indicate that it may not in practice be possible to deal fully with all such contingencies in advance.

B. SERVICES

If a joint venture is located in the plant or offices of one of the participants, its economic operation may well, as stated earlier, depend on the continuing supply of office, administrative and other services on pre-agreed or possibly pre-existing terms. A different kind of problem arises where the joint venture is, at any rate in its initial stages, intended to combine the participants' development efforts in a certain field. Where the joint venture depends on the development resources of the participants, it must be in a position to obtain these on terms settled in advance in a manner rather analogous to the supply of equipment. Where it is to carry out the development effort for the benefit of the participants, then again it must be able to obtain appropriate reimbursement from them on a continuing basis. In the case of a joint development, there will also clearly be need for a careful definition of the joint venture's and participants' intellectual property rights arising directly and indirectly from that development (see p. 70).

Often, particularly in the early stages of its development, a joint venture will depend on the provision of key personnel, possibly on a loan basis, by one or other participant. In such cases the parties must address themselves in detail to the question of whether these people remain employees of the loaning participant, who is responsible for local taxes, social security payments, etc., and perhaps more particularly who has the power to decide over their retention or otherwise. The problems are not in principle different from those arising when employees are provided to help the purchaser of a major project to get it established but they are certainly manifold and, where they can arise, repay careful study.

C. INTELLECTUAL PROPERTY RIGHTS

In all cases where a joint venture depends on patents, know-how, copyright or trade marks of the participants, there will have to be agreements covering these matters. Likewise, the joint venture may itself generate intellectual property rights to which the participants will require access.

Due to the fact that control over a joint venture is shared – and indeed may be shared with parties of widely differing backgrounds and with diametrically-opposed interests – details of the grant of intellectual property rights become very important, particularly their territorial scope and the degree of exclusivity attached to them. These requirements may vary between different classes of industrial property, e.g. the right to use patents compared, say, to access to know-how. The right of the licensor to improvements, assignability and flow-back, as well as the post-agreement position, require spelling out. The points at issue do not differ from those calling for consideration in any arm's length licensing deal but they may well have a special sensitivity in relation to legal restraints on anti-competitive agreements mentioned on p. 97. Failure to deal adequately with intellectual property rights can lead to fragmentation of rights, particularly if the joint venturers continue to use the rights in parallel with the joint venture. This can give rise to difficulties in effecting registrations and subsequent enforcement of rights.

These matters require particular attention in relation to the situation which can arise when, for any reason, the joint venture comes to an end. A party which has made an important contribution to the joint venture might then find itself cut off from the technology to which it has contributed. It is here that subsidiary and contingent agreements between the participants may need to be created to avoid an unbalanced and inequitable result. In fact, where one participant would, for whatever reason, enjoy considerable advantage over the other in the event of a termination of the joint venture, this may well become an inducement to find grounds for termination.

An important question in this context is the extent of any flow-back rights, i.e. the rights of the participants on termination to any improvements made by the joint venture to the intellectual property licensed to it. It is not always straightforward to allocate development which has taken place in a joint venture clearly to the contribution made by one or other party. Here again, much will depend on the purposes for which the joint venture is created. Where a joint venture exists only for the purposes of manufacturing items and supplying them to the joint venturers, then certainly at least for a reasonable time after termination either joint venturer must have the right to use the relevant intellectual property rights of the other to the extent that they had been available to the joint venture, as well as those of the joint venture itself.

It should be emphasized that the content of any licence agreement will in practice be strongly determined by any relevant anti-trust legislation. In some circumstances the controlling bodies may themselves wish to ensure continuing rights for participants on termination of a joint venture. These matters will be looked at more fully in Part IV.

Chapter 9

Termination and Admission of New Parties

In some circumstances a Shareholders' Agreement becomes redundant the moment the operation is in place (see Chapter 7). If this is the case, it should be stated in the agreement. However, in most cases there will be continuing obligations under that agreement, if only in respect of mutual confidentiality.

Where the joint venture is for a specific purpose, that purpose will govern the termination of the relationship. If parties have jointly tendered and their tender has been rejected, then, apart possibly from some confidentiality undertakings, the relationship will be at an end. If the tender has been accepted and the project has run to completion, including any warranty period, then again the relationship will normally be brought to an end.

The case of a joint venture for indefinite duration is more complex and the complexity grows with the number of interrelated agreements. A party, by not meeting future capital requirements, may reduce its stake in the joint venture to a point where it is no longer equitable that it should have full control rights (see also p. 62). On the other hand, it will, in such circumstances, not wish to lose control and remain locked in. It is therefore conceivable that the other party can demand the transfer to it of the first party's shareholding, or that it can abrogate the agreement, leaving it to the party whose stake has diminished to dispose of its shareholding on a pre-agreed basis, if it so wishes. The permutations are manifold.

As regards the agreements between parties and the joint venture, their duration and termination periods may vary from subject to subject so that, for example, an agreement for services is subject to a much shorter notice period than a licence of intellectual property rights, which may be basic to the future existence of the joint venture.[1] When a party pulls out of the joint venture, it will be important for the joint venture not to lose any intellectual property rights it has already acquired, but redefinition of the future relationship may be necessary, both as regards improvements introduced by the participant and as regards his flow-back rights from the joint venture. Needless to say, other considerations again arise on dissolution of the joint venture itself.

Where the name of the joint venture carries an association with any of the parties it is common for there to be a requirement for the name to be changed if that party ceases to be a participant to one which carries no such connotation. This is unlikely to be controversial.

There are no simple rules for this but these remarks should indicate that these topics have to be addressed at the drafting and negotiating stage since failure to do so can bring about totally unintended results.

As already indicated on p. 51, similar problems arise when a shareholding in a corporate joint venture is to be transferred to a new participant or one is to be admitted in addition. The variety of possible situations will normally be too great for all the consequences to be spelled out when the joint venture is created, i.e. before the accession of a new party is even considered. It is important to assure that not only the rights and obligations of the new participant are clearly in mind, but also that those of the former participants do not bring about surprise situations, particularly in regard to continuing access to technology.

Despite the foregoing it will be clear that for many reasons the situation on termination of a joint venture may not have been spelled out either at all, or only incompletely, in the initial documentation. This is particularly true of joint ventures which are expected to exist for at any rate as long as all participants are in business. In such cases it will usually be in the interests of both parties at the time of termination to enter into a termination agreement or a series of such agreements dealing with as many of the matters covered in the preceding chapters as may be appropriate in the circumstances. That even such a series of agreements cannot guarantee the absence of any future discord is well illustrated by the case of *BICC plc v Burnby Corp. and Another* reported in [1985] 1 All ER 417.

---

1 For a set of joint venture agreements for varying periods, see the Notice of the EEC Commission concerning Rockwell International Corporation and Iveco Industrial Corporation BV in [1982] 2 CMLR 565

Chapter 10

Liability of the Joint Venturers to Each Other and to the Joint Venture

The conflict of interest which may arise between a participant and a joint venture or between the participants has already been mentioned on p. 27. Particularly in an unincorporated joint venture one of the parties may often be involved in dealing on behalf of all parties. Typically conflicts of interest may arise when there is actual or potential competition between participants or between one or more of them and the joint venture, or where the parties have a relationship arising from the supply of goods and/or services. Directors and executives who are appointed or seconded to the joint venture, as well as other loaned personnel, are exposed to this problem and a management contract given to one participant raises it in acute form.

These matters cannot normally be dealt with comprehensively in agreements and must therefore be considered under the laws applicable to the particular situation. They are likely to involve questions of agency and of fiduciary trust. As regards the latter, it has long been recognized in the US that joint venturers must be expected to act in a fiduciary capacity towards each other for so long as the joint venture between them continues (see p. xiii)[1] and the application of this principle to joint ventures has been restated by C. J. Goetz and R. E. Scott in 'Principles of relational contracts' in 67 (1981) *Virginia Law Review* pp. 1089 et seq. (1126). In Australia, where there appear to be many contractual joint ventures in the mining and petroleum exploration field and the volume

---

1 See Zaphiriou, p. 249.

of legal discussion of this topic is extremely high,[2] the court in a recent case extended this burden to circumstances where a joint venture was only in contemplation between the parties.[3]

In English law the liability for breach of fiduciary duty by one of the joint venturers appeared to be rather less certain. In the case of *Multinational Gas and Petrochemical Company* v *Multinational Gas and Petrochemical Services Ltd and Others* [1983] 2 All ER 563 and commented upon in (1984) 49 *MLR* 87, the liquidator of an insolvent Liberian company sought unsuccessfully to recover damages against its shareholders and an advisory company, but the case concerns only the question of service out of the jurisdiction. Nevertheless, the *Modern Law Review* at 88 states that shareholders in a joint venture, unlike directors, do not owe it fiduciary duty.

The later case of *Elliott* v *Wheeldon* [1993] BCLC 53 is, however, more positive on the rights of joint venturers against one another and specifically confirms that certain duties of joint venturers to one another can exist where the parties agree to carry on a joint venture through the medium of a company, particularly if the relationship has the characteristics of a partnership. A US case, *Essex Chemical Corporation* v *Gurit-Heberlein A.G.* 857 F2d 1463 (3rd Circuit, 1988),[4] in which one joint venturer had made a takeover bid for his co-venturer, appears to have been settled prior to final judgment. It and related cases are discussed by D. M. Cendali and R. E. Juceam in the *Journal of Proprietary Rights* in December 1989 and January 1990.

Another relevant case is *Hanson* v *Lorenz & Jones and Others* reported in (1986) 136 *NLJ* 1088. In this case the defendant solicitors had advised on the creation of a joint venture in the property field between the plaintiff and a financing company in which the solicitors had an undisclosed financial interest and which in turn placed a building contract, admittedly on a tender basis, with a building firm in which they also had an undisclosed interest. From the details available it may be inferred that the plaintiff had suffered no real damage and was only attacking the plaintiffs out of spite in order to recover the fees paid to them. Nevertheless the judgment in favour of the solicitors does not

---

2 Particular reference should be made to the *Australian Mining and Petroleum Law Journal* and its successor, the *Australian Mining and Petroleum Law Association Yearbook*.
3 *Brian Pty Ltd* v *United Dominions Corporation Ltd* (1983) 1 NSWLR 490 at 505.
4 For a full review see Michael Lower in JBL 1994, 507ss.

appear to give the legal advisers' fiduciary duty much support. All this suggests again that the parties to incorporated and unincorporated joint ventures should pay particular attention to the likelihood of any acts in the future which could bring them into conflict with each other and/or with the joint venture and should try to anticipate in their contracts at least the more obvious cases of future discord.

PART III

ACCOUNTING AND TAXATION

Chapter 11

Accounting and Taxation Aspects[1]

ACCOUNTING ASPECTS

Although the details will vary from one jurisdiction to another, certain principles relating to the accounting treatment of joint ventures have gained international acceptance and have been incorporated, with minor variations, in accounting standards around the world.

These principles recognize three possible scenarios:

(i) A passive investment

Where the participant does not exercise significant influence over the joint venture's affairs, the investment should be carried at cost in the participant's group accounts and income recognized only as and when received by the participant. There is a presumption that a participant does not exercise significant influence where the participant's ownership of the joint venture amounts to 20 per cent or less. Of course, a participant with a holding of less than 20 per cent may not be a joint venturer in the true sense.

(ii) An associated undertaking

An associated undertaking exists where the participant has a participating interest in the undertaking held on a long-term basis and the participant exercises a significant influence over that undertaking but it is not a subsidiary. Where an associated undertaking exists, equity accounting is appropriate. As many joint ventures are likely to fall into

---

1 *Joint ventures, an Accounting, Tax and Administrative Guide* (1987) by Joseph K. Morris, CPA, deals with these matters comprehensively from a US point of view.

this category, the requirements of equity accounting are discussed in more detail below.

(iii) A subsidiary

Where the participant's interest amounts to more than 50 per cent, or where the joint venture is required to be treated by the participant as a subsidiary for other reasons (e.g. by virtue of the degree of control it is able to exercise), full consolidation is appropriate (as with any other subsidiary).

It should be noted that, whilst the boundary between a subsidiary and an associated undertaking is generally legally defined, the boundary between an associated undertaking and a passive investment tends to be more fluid. In the UK, there is a rebuttable presumption that significant influence (and therefore the relationship of associated undertaking) exists where there is a holding of 20 per cent or more.

EQUITY ACCOUNTING

As might be expected, equity accounting is an attempt to find a compromise between the treatment accorded to a passive investment and full consolidation. The principle of equity accounting is that the participant group's share of net earnings is recognized in the consolidated profit and loss account and in the balance sheet the carrying value of the investment is lifted by the retained portion of the participant group's share of net earnings. The essential difference between equity accounting and full consolidation is therefore that under equity accounting the relevant information is shown as a net item whereas in consolidated accounts the relevant figures for the parent company and its subsidiary undertakings are aggregated, subject to appropriate adjustments.

PROPORTIONAL CONSOLIDATION

The European Union's Seventh Company Law Directive on Consolidation Accounts 83/349/EEC allows proportional consolidation as an option which Member States may make available if they wish as an alternative to equity accounting for joint ventures. Under proportional consolidation, the participant group's share of each item of assets, liabilities, income and expenses is consolidated on a line-by-line basis. In addition, certain limited information about the joint venture is required to be disclosed in notes to the accounts. Member States have implemented this part of the Seventh Directive in different ways. In the UK, the use of proportional consolidation is limited by law to unincorporated joint ventures. Germany permits a participant to use proportional consolidation in relation to a holding in a joint venture company provided that the other participant(s) do not consolidate. In France, by contrast, a participant must use proportional consolidation where there is joint control, which in this context is understood as meaning where a decision on an important matter cannot be taken without the consent of the other participant(s). In the US, the rules on the use of proportional consolidation are even more restrictive than in the UK.[2]

It should be noted that the above requirements apply to the consolidated accounts of the participant's group. In the participant company's own accounts, the joint venture should be carried at cost as for a passive investment and income recognized only as and when received.

Where the joint venture's accounts show a deficit, the treatment in the participant's group accounts will depend on whether the joint venture is incorporated or unincorporated. In the case of an unincorporated joint venture, it will be necessary to show the deficiency in full. Where the joint venture is incorporated, the equity investment may generally be written off together with any loans made by the participant to the joint venture. However, this would not be appropriate where there is a continuing intention by the participant to support the joint venture. In that case, the deficit and an appropriate allowance for anticipated future losses should be shown in the parent's accounts as a contingent liability.

---

2 The Accounting Standards Board in the UK has recently issued an exposure draft containing revised proposals for changes to the accounting requirements for joint ventures entitled 'FRED 11 Associates and Joint Ventures'. If implemented in their present form, these proposals would permit proportional consolidation for corporate joint ventures where each joint venturer is economically interested in specific assets and liabilities, but not others. The Department of Trade and Industry has indicated that it would be willing to amend company law to allow corporate joint ventures to use proportional consolidation in these circumstances. Other significant changes contemplated by FRED 11 include clarification of the distinction between a passive investment and an associate undertaking in order to achieve greater consistency.

TAXATION

The tax analysis of the setting up and operation of most joint ventures is likely to be quite complex and will be influenced by many considerations, including the nature of the participants' contributions, the nature of the joint venture's business, the territories involved and the participants' own circumstances. It follows that no two cases will be identical but, in most situations, it is likely that some or all of the following issues will need to be considered:

(a) Losses

It is often the case that the joint venture will incur losses during the early stages. If a non-corporate structure is used, it is probable that the participants will be able to claim immediate relief for these losses against their own current profits. Where a limited liability company is used as the joint venture vehicle, the participants' ability to obtain relief on losses incurred by the joint venture may be much more restricted. In some situations, it may be possible to establish the joint venture as a subsidiary of one of the parties for tax purposes, but still maintain joint control.[3] This will enable one of the participants to claim group benefits, but not the other(s). It would therefore be normal for the shareholders' agreement to provide for any relief transferred either to or from the joint venture company to be purchased at full consideration.

It is more probable that the joint venture will not qualify as a subsidiary of any of the joint venturers for tax purposes. In that case, local legislation may permit a proportion of trading losses to be relieved. In the UK, for example, 'consortium relief' is available under Chapter IV of the Taxes Act 1988 where at least three-quarters of a UK tax resident company's ordinary share capital is beneficially owned by a consortium of UK tax resident companies, none of which beneficially owns less than 5 per cent or 75 per cent or more of the ordinary share capital.[4]

---

3 See *J. Sainsbury* v *O'Connor (Inspector of Taxes)* [1991] STC 318, but see also p. 87 below.

4 In *ICI* v *Colmer (Inspector of Taxes)* [1993] STC 710 it was held that it was possible for a UK trading company to surrender losses to its immediate holding company, and thence to its ultimate parents, even though the majority of the holding company's subsidiaries were non-UK tax resident. In that case the two ultimate parents constituted a 'consortium' for the purposes of Part IV of the 1988 Act.

UK consortium relief is not allowed where connected persons control or have the ability to control 75 per cent or more of a company's voting rights. Persons are treated as connected where there are two or more persons acting to secure or exercise control of a company. In *Steele (Inspector of Taxes)* v *EVC International NV* [1996] STC 785 two shareholders in a joint venture company were treated as connected where it was found that they had acted together and exercised control by performing their obligations under the Shareholders' Agreement between them and voting at general meetings in the manner required by the Shareholders' Agreement. This decision would appear to have significant implications for UK joint ventures where the parties intend to claim consortium relief.

(b) Put and Call Options

In *Sainsbury's case* quoted above the English courts gave effect to a put and call option arrangement which enabled one shareholder to become a 30 per cent shareholder in due course whilst permitting the other shareholder to establish a 75 per cent shareholding and claim group relief in the meantime. Following that case, Schedule 18 of the Taxes Act 1988 was amended to provide that where such options exist it will be assumed in determining the companies' relationships for tax purposes that they have been exercised. This anti-avoidance provision is likely to have a significant impact on a joint venture being established in the UK where put or call options are contemplated.

(c) The Participants' Contributions

Where a business or assets are being transferred into the joint venture, two options are likely to be available: either the participant could transfer the asset(s) themselves to the joint venture; or the shares in the company which owns the relevant asset(s) could be transferred. The choice between these options is likely to depend largely on tax considerations such as the treatment of any capital gains arising, the effect on tax depreciation (capital) allowances, potential liability to Value Added Tax on the transfer, stamp and capital duty charges and so on. Of course, if a purely contractual joint venture is used there may be no transfer of assets by the participants to the joint venture and these issues will not arise.

(d) Distribution of Profits

An important difference generally between an incorporated joint venture and a joint venture carried on through a non-corporate structure (i.e. a contractual joint venture or a partnership) is that under a non-corporate structure the profits will accrue directly to the participants whereas under a corporate structure the participants would normally receive profits by way of dividends. The tax treatment of dividends is likely to give rise to an additional layer of complication.

(e) Cross-border Joint Ventures

Where a joint venture is established to carry on business in a number of jurisdictions, the most appropriate structure will frequently be to establish a network of trading subsidiaries in the relevant jurisdictions under the ownership of a jointly owned holding company. In such a situation, it is desirable to locate the holding company in a territory with a low rate of corporate taxation, but which also has favourable double taxation treaties with the other countries involved.

(f) Transactions with the Joint Venturers

It is probable that the joint venture will enter into one or more contracts with the participants, involving (inter alia) the use of intellectual property, the supply of goods or services and so on. Where such arrangements are entered into other than on arms' length terms, anti-avoidance legislation may permit the local tax authorities to substitute the market value for tax purposes. This is sometimes known as 'transfer pricing'.

(g) Tax Depreciation (Capital) Allowances

Where the joint venture is expected to make a profit soon after its formation, tax depreciation (or capital) allowances may be available on initial expenditure on those fixed assets of the business consisting of plant and machinery. In such a situation, it may be possible to 'gear up' the benefit of the capital allowances by financing the joint venture through a combination of equity and debt. However, such arrangements should be carefully structured to avoid challenge by the tax authorities. In the UK case of *Ensign Tankers (Leasing) v Stokes (Inspector of Taxes)* [1992] STC 226, a limited recourse loan under which the borrower's obligation to repay was limited to film receipts was held to be a disguised joint venture between the borrower and the lender. Accordingly, a proportion of the capital allowances claimed corresponding to the amount contributed by the lender was disallowed.

(h) Repatriation of Profits

International joint ventures should be structured so as to minimize the risk that the participants will be liable twice for tax on the same income and capital gains. This problem is particularly severe in the case of countries which, like the UK, have an imputation system of taxation.[5] In the UK, a company is obliged to account for Advance Corporation Tax ('ACT') on dividend payments. A UK resident shareholder will receive a tax credit in relation to the ACT, but a foreign shareholder with no other income in the UK will frequently not be able to make use of the tax credit.

These difficulties can be overcome by the use of 'income access' arrangements. For example, two parties resident in territories A and B respectively wish to establish a joint venture in territory C, which will own their businesses in territories A and B. The joint venture is structured so that the trading companies in territories A and B are subsidiaries of the joint venture vehicle, but each of the joint venturers is issued with an 'income access share' in the local subsidiary. Dividends in respect of the local operation are paid direct from the local subsidiary to the participant, bypassing the subsidiary's immediate holding company, with equalization payments between the participants to balance any difference in profitability/distribution between the trading companies. The income access shares are 'stapled' to the participant's shares in the joint venture so that they cannot be held by separate owners. For a diagram illustrating such a structure see Appendix IIC.

(i) Value Added Tax

In jurisdictions which operate a system of value added (or similar) tax (VAT), it will be necessary to consider whether the joint venture

---

5 Countries which, at the time of writing, operate an imputation system include Australia, Belgium, Canada, Finland, France, Germany, Gibraltar, Ireland, Italy, Malaysia, New Zealand, Norway, Singapore, Thailand and the UK. There is a general trend for countries to move towards an imputation system, but the US, which has retained a classical system, is a notable exception.

constitutes a separate entity for VAT purposes. European joint ventures can be the subject of certain beneficial VAT treatment in some territories provided that the appropriate clearance is obtained.

(j) Cross-border Non-corporate Joint Ventures

The tax treatment of cross-border non-corporate joint ventures operating in different jurisdictions is likely to be quite complex. In particular, the participants should appreciate that they might be treated as carrying on business in each jurisdiction in which the joint venture operates, which is probably something they would prefer to avoid.

Certain tax issues which should be borne in mind when considering how a joint venture should be structured are dealt with in Chapter 7.

PART IV

LEGAL RESTRAINTS AND REGULATION

Chapter 12

Regulatory Controls

Like any other business, a joint venture is likely to be subject to many different kinds of governmental control and regulation. However, there are certain types of regulation which are particularly relevant to joint ventures. The following affect only international joint ventures and are concerned with the regulation of foreign investment in a country.

FOREIGN INVESTMENT REGULATIONS

Sometimes foreign investment controls will prohibit outright ownership of an undertaking by a foreigner, but investment in a joint venture with a local partner may be permitted. A joint venture would then be the only option available to a foreign company wishing to enter that particular market. At the time of writing, restrictions of this sort are becoming less common as more and more countries in the former communist bloc and the developing world open their borders to foreign investment. However, such restrictions are still likely to be encountered in situations where national interests are perceived to be affected, such as the defence industry, telecommunications, broadcasting and other industries of strategic national importance.

Within the European Union it has become difficult for Member States' governments to limit investment by nationals of other Member States as this may infringe the provisions of the Treaty of Rome relating to the freedom of establishment and prohibition of discrimination on the grounds of nationality.[1] In 1990–91 the UK Government ran into conflict with the European Commission over its policy towards

---

1 Articles 52–58 and Article 6 of the Treaty of Rome.

take-overs by State-owned or controlled companies. Concerned at the prospect of what he described as 'nationalization by the back door', the UK Secretary of State for Trade and Industry announced in July 1990 that he would, in future, pay particularly close attention to the degree of State control of the acquiring company in deciding whether to refer a merger to the Monopolies and Mergers Commission.[2] In the following months, five cases involving take-overs by State-owned EC companies were referred to the MMC, all of which were French. Following a complaint to the Commission by one of those companies, Crédit Lyonnais, the UK Government was subsequently required to clarify its policy in this area, and in an exchange of letters between the UK Government and the European Commission published on 30 October 1991 the UK Government confirmed that the fact that a bidder was State-owned or directed by the State 'would not *per se* justify a referral to the MMC'. A referral would be envisaged only where public interest issues (such as security) arose or where there were competition issues.

FOREIGN EXCHANGE CONTROL REGULATIONS

In certain markets, where the investment itself is permitted, it may still be subject to exchange control regulations which limit or restrict the remittance of profits, royalties, and management charges and the repatriation of capital, whether in the form of return on equity or loan payments. In some circumstances, it may be possible to obtain a waiver of any restrictions in advance from the relevant authorities, or at least obtain their approval to the terms of the proposed investment including the terms on which funds will be repatriated. The foreign investor may be able to take out investment insurance against breach of any

---

2 Under the Fair Trading Act 1973 the Secretary of State has a discretion to refer a case to the Monopolies and Mergers Commission where there is 'a merger situation qualifying for investigation' under s 64. The MMC must then prepare a report for the Secretary of State on the proposed merger and make recommendations. The Secretary of State is not bound by any recommendations in the report and has wide ranging powers, including, inter alia, the power to prevent the merger going ahead.

undertakings given by the host government.[3] However, it should be noted that insurance will not normally cover the foreign investor against the failure to grant such undertakings in the first place. The making of the investment should therefore be conditional upon any required undertakings being granted.

Far more complex is governmental regulation of restrictive practices or monopoly control. The complexity arises largely from the fact that the territorial boundaries of such legislation are more loosely defined and, for example in the case of the EU, there is often a two-tier system in place. When this is coupled with the fact that the different authorities and legislations have different objectives and, therefore, have different rules and apply different criteria, then the complexity becomes apparent. This subject is discussed in more detail in the following chapter.

---

3 Investment insurance may be available from the Export Credit Agency in the foreign investor's home territory or the private market. The kind of risks commonly covered by investment insurance include expropriation (i.e. nationalization), compulsory acquisition or confiscation of assets by the host government, discriminatory measures by the host government against the joint venture and physical damage and operational losses caused by war or revolution.

Chapter 13

Competition Law Aspects

In their different ways, the laws of countries which concern themselves with control over anti-competitive activities have tended to look at joint ventures as *prima facie* restricting competition. This may be partly due to the legal nature of joint ventures, which in most jurisdictions do not have a legal form peculiar to themselves. Thus, in the absence of alternatives, the procedure for evaluating the legality of joint ventures from an anti-trust point of view is frequently the same as that used for analysing mergers and acquisitions.[1]

It is easy to see other reasons why joint ventures might be regarded as anti-competitive:

— where two competitors join up in marketing a particular product in a country they have excluded the possibility that they will each enter that market separately;

— an agreement for joint procurement can strengthen the parties' hold on available supplies of raw materials or intermediates;

— a joint manufacturing agreement can lead to a dominant position in the market for the production in question;

— joint development can be seen as inherently restrictive of competition because the parties will not pursue development of the same product independently.

The controlling authorities sometimes tend to read into joint venture agreements restrictions on the freedom of the individual joint venturers, even where they are not expressly spelled out. They will also, particularly in regard to businesses which are competitors in a

---

1 See *United States v Penn-Olin Chemical Co.*, 378, US 158, 170 (1964).

substantial way, be suspicious that the joint venture may be a covert substitute for market-sharing arrangements.[2] The object and effects of the joint venture will therefore be assessed by regulators in terms of the restriction of actual or potential competition between the participants themselves, between the participants and the joint venture and between all of the above and third party competitors, suppliers and purchasers so that ultimately its effect on the market in question can be determined.

In many cases, the participants are not competitors when they enter into the joint venture. Even then the controlling body or bodies tend to be concerned with the fact that in the absence of the joint venture there might have been a probability, or at least a possibility, that they would have become competitors. To put it another way, if it is reasonable to assume that in the absence of the joint venture the participants would have gone into the business separately, the *prima facie* inference will be that there is a restriction of competition. The extent to which this assumption can be rebutted will depend on the circumstances and the legislation in question.

In most jurisdictions the authorities tend to view collaborative research and development as benign on the basis that, in the absence of the joint arrangements, the parties are unlikely to have been prepared to carry out the development separately – see, for example, the National Co-operative Research Act 1984 in the US. Downstream collaboration in the market place on the other hand is more likely to attract critical attention from the regulatory authorities.

The formal organization of a joint venture will not usually be of primary concern to the controlling authorities. In general, they will apply the same criteria to a contractual joint venture as to a corporate one and will be concerned with its anti-competitive aspects regardless of form, although a joint venture related to a single project will obviously be allowed more easily than a joint venture of indefinite duration.[3] However, there are instances where the formal position can be significant. In the UK, for example, it may be possible to structure the arrangements in such a way that the parties are not obliged to furnish

---

2 See, e.g. Mok pp. 131–133. A Common Market case which attracted much attention is that of *Irish Distillers Group* v *G.C. & C. Brands Limited* (1988) 4 CMLR 840, in which three leading drinks companies had set up a joint venture to acquire a competitor and to establish a market sharing agreement.
3 See, e.g. *Re Eurotunnel* (1988) 4 CMLR 746.

details to the Office of Fair Trading under the Restrictive Trade Practices Act 1976. Similarly, it may be possible to adjust the parties' rights and obligations so as to take a transaction outside the EU Merger Regulation if this is felt to be desirable.

In reviewing a joint venture, the controlling authorities will generally look not just at the main agreement but at all related ones to arrive at an overall view. A long-term supply agreement which is an integral part of a joint venture may be objectionable. Even where there is no formal supply agreement but supply to the parties is implied, the European Commission, in particular, may well look at the effect on the market to which that supply relates (the so-called 'foreclosure' effect). The European Union has also established rules which aim to restrict the use of patent and know-how licences as well as distribution agreements to create separate national markets in the individual countries under the guise of industrial property rights, etc. The Community also seeks to ensure that on termination of the joint venture for whatever reason, one party is not, as a result of these agreements, eliminated as a future competitor.

When dealing with joint ventures with an international dimension it will frequently be necessary to examine the impact of the laws of each of the territories affected by the joint venture. This will not necessarily be limited to those countries where the joint venture has a physical presence, particularly in the case of transactions which have some connection with the United States. In the words of the US Department of Justice:

> 'The reach of the US anti-trust laws is not limited to conduct and transactions that occur within the boundaries of the United States. Anti-competitive conduct that affects US domestic or foreign commerce may violate the US anti-trust laws regardless of where such conduct occurs or the nationality of the parties involved.'[4]

Furthermore, in *Hartford Fire Insurance Co v California* 113 S.Ct. 2891, 2909 (1993) the US Supreme Court stated that, where a transaction is subject to both US anti-trust law and the competition laws of another jurisdiction, a party will, where possible, be required to comply with the laws of both jurisdictions. A party could therefore find itself in breach of

---

4 'Department of Justice and Federal Trade Commission Antitrust Enforcement Guidelines for International Operations', 5 April 1995.

US law, even though it has already complied with all relevant laws of the territory where the joint venture is situated.

THE EU MERGER REGULATION

In assessing the legality of joint ventures in the European Union, it was, in the past, necessary to consider both the impact of Community law and the legislation of the relevant Member States. This caused considerable complexity and, in some cases, uncertainty as to the legality of transactions, but in 1989 the Council of the European Communities passed the Merger Control Regulation which alleviated some of these difficulties, although other problems remain.

The Merger Regulation,[5] which came into effect in September 1990, has had a significant impact on joint ventures. Following the introduction of the Merger Regulation, EU competition law distinguishes between 'concentrative joint ventures having a community dimension', which fall to be considered under the Merger Regulation, and 'co-operative joint ventures', to which Article 85 of the Treaty of Rome continues to apply (see p. 100 below). A concentrative joint venture is defined under Article 3(2) of the Merger Regulation as 'a joint venture performing on a lasting basis all the functions of an autonomous economic entity which does not give rise to co-ordination of the competitive behaviour of the parties amongst themselves or between them and the joint venture'. The Merger Regulation only applies to concentrative joint ventures 'having a community dimension'. This second test is designed to ensure that only large-scale concentrations significantly affecting more than one Member State are caught.[6] In addition, a joint venture will only fall to be considered under the Merger

---

5 Council Regulation (EEC) No. 4064/89 of 21 December 1989 on the Control of Concentrations between Undertakings.

6 A concentration will be treated as having a community dimension if the following conditions are satisfied:

    (1) The aggregate world-wide turnover of all the undertakings concerned must exceed ECU 5 billion (approximately US$6.25 billion);

    (2) At least two of the undertakings involved must each have an aggregate community-wide turnover of ECU 250 million (approximately US$310 million); and

Regulation if it is controlled by one of the parties or there is joint control between a number of the participants.

The logic of the Merger Regulation is that concentrations which are intended to bring about a lasting change in the structure of the industry concerned should be treated differently from arrangements which have the effect of co-ordinating the competitive behaviour of undertakings which remain independent. If a joint venture falls within the Merger Regulation then, subject to certain limited exceptions, Member States are precluded from applying their own competition laws to the transaction. The transaction must be notified to the Commission's Merger Task Force and there is a clear timetable for review of the transaction by the Merger Task Force to assess whether it is compatible with the Common Market. Broadly speaking a transaction will be compatible with the Common Market provided that it satisfies the requirements for consideration under the Merger Regulation and does not 'create or strengthen a dominant position as a result of which effective competition would be significantly impeded in the Common Market or in a substantial part of it'. This is a somewhat less rigorous test than that under Article 85(1) (see below). If the Merger Task Force clears the transaction, no further authorizations are needed under Article 85 or Article 86 of the Treaty of Rome or under the domestic law of any Member State (the so-called 'one-stop shop'). If the joint venture itself is found not to infringe the Merger Regulation, any ancillary restrictions will also be cleared, provided that they are directly related and necessary to the implementation of the concentration, i.e. the concentration cannot be disassociated from the restriction without jeopardizing its existence.[7] Such restrictions cannot later be challenged under Article 85(1).

---

(3) The concentration will not have a Community dimension if each of the undertakings concerned achieves more than two-thirds of its aggregate community-wide turnover in one and the same Member State.

A transaction which falls below these thresholds, or in respect of which the requirements of paragraph (3) are satisfied, would be dealt with under Article 85 and the relevant Member States' national laws with the result that the parties may be required to make filings in a number of Member States. Periodic attempts by the Commission to extend its competence by lowering the thresholds have met with concerted resistance from certain Member States wishing to preserve their own jurisdiction in this area.

7 Commission Notice regarding restrictions ancillary to concentrations (90/C 203/05).

There is now a short form procedure for notifications under the Merger Regulation for joint ventures where the turnover of the joint venture in the EEA is less than ECU 100 million (US$125 million) and the total value of the assets contributed to the joint venture is also less than ECU 100 million.

ARTICLES 85 AND 86 OF THE TREATY OF ROME

Joint ventures which do not fall within the Merger Regulation remain subject to the provisions of Articles 85 and 86 and, where relevant, the applicable Member State's national competition law. Article 85(1) prohibits as incompatible with the Common Market all agreements, decisions and concerted practices which have as their object or effect the prevention, restriction or distortion of competition within the Common Market and which may affect trade between Member States. Article 86 prohibits any abuse by one or more undertakings of a dominant position within the Common Market or a substantial part of it. Under Article 85, there is no mandatory requirement for the transaction to be notified to the Commission, but if the transaction falls within the provisions of Article 85(1), which are very broad, it will be prohibited unless specifically exempt. Exemption can be obtained in one of a number of ways: an application may be made for an individual exemption under Article 85(3) or for negative clearance (i.e. a decision from the Commission confirming that the transaction falls outside Article 85(1)) or attempts may be made to bring the transaction within one of the 'block exemptions' granted by the Commission in relation to specific activities. Alternatively, the joint venture may fall within the Commission's Notice on Agreements of Minor Importance.[8] The length of time taken to obtain exemption or negative clearance under Article 85 is much longer than the corresponding procedure under the Merger Regulation, typically

---

8 Commission Notice of 3 September 1986 on agreements of minor importance which do not fall under Article 85(1) of the Treaty establishing the European Economic Community [O J 1986] C23 1/2. This Notice, which is not binding on the Commission, exempts from Article 85(1) transactions where the goods or services concerned do not represent more than 5 per cent of the total market for such goods or services in the area of the Common Market affected by the agreement and the aggregate turnover of all the participants does not exceed ECU 200 million (approximately US$250 million).

around two years. The Commission has recently introduced a fast-track procedure for so-called structural joint ventures, but this will not apply to all cases. A case can be dealt with more quickly if the parties are prepared to accept a non-legally binding comfort letter from the Commission, but this may not be a perfect solution (see the *Guerlain* case below).

In fact, if a joint venture is clearly inoffensive, e.g. because it has no material effect on trade between Member States, then Article 85(1) is considered inapplicable. Where it does apply and the joint venturers decide to seek exemption under Article 85(3), it will be necessary to show a benefit to the user as likely to result from their project. For instance, in a market dominated by one supplier it may be that a joint venture between two smaller parties will have the effect of improving rather than restricting competition. In practice, a joint venture which is cleared under Article 85 is unlikely to be caught under Article 86.

As in the United States, common research and, in certain circumstances, product development and specialization in manufacture, rank for exemption more readily than projects involving downstream collaboration,[9] particularly if they are covered by block exemptions adopted by the EEC on 19 December 1984 (Regulation 418/85). Many exemptions under Article 85(3) are given subject to a time-limit, but, providing the conditions have been adhered to, that time-limit will be appropriately extended.[10]

The position under Member States' national law may vary depending on which of these options applies. In the *Guerlain* case involving the distribution of perfume, various French perfume manufacturers were successfully prosecuted for breaches of French national competition law after the Commission had issued a comfort letter stating that it had no further grounds for intervening under Article 85. An application was made to the European Court of Justice on the grounds that the French national authorities could not prohibit under national law restrictions which had been recognized as lawful under Community law. The application failed on the basis that comfort letters did not constitute exemption under Article 85(3) but merely an administrative decision by

---

9 See, e.g. *Re Carbon Gas Technologie GmbH* (1984) 2 CMLR 275; *Continental Gummi-Werke and Michelin et Cie* (1988) 4 CMLR 677; and *General Electric Company plc and others* (1988) 4 CMLR 815.
10 See, e.g. *Re Laval-Stork VOF* (1988) 4 CMLR 714.

the Commission not to pursue the case. In the UK, section 5(1) of the Restrictive Trade Practices Act 1976 expressly states that the Act will continue to apply notwithstanding that the agreement in question may be exempted under Article 85(3) of the EU Treaty. However, in practice, the UK authorities will not usually take action under the Restrictive Trade Practices Act if an application has been made to the Commission under Article 85(3) and the Commission has either granted exemption or issued a comfort letter.

SANCTIONS

The powers of a regulatory authority in relation to a particular transaction, and the sanctions applicable for breach of anti-trust laws, will normally be set out in the relevant legislation. The possible range of sanctions would include:

   (1) an order requiring that the deal be unscrambled. Where the implementation of the joint venture involved the acquisition of an existing business, its divesture would then be required (UK Fair Trading Act 1973);

   (2) the imposition of fines[11] (Articles 85 and 86) or even, in the US, imprisonment (Sherman Act (15 U.S.C. 1));

   (3) an order restraining the parties from giving effect to the offending restrictions (UK Restrictive Trade Practices Act 1976);

   (4) an order prohibiting the parties from going ahead with the transaction (Merger Regulation).

In addition, a third party which can show that it has suffered loss as a result of the contravention may be able to recover damages from the joint venture parties. This is the case, for example, under Article 85 of the Treaty of Rome. See *Garden Cottage Foods v Milk Marketing Board* [1984] AC 130, [1983] 3 CMLR 43.

Thus, whilst in some instances, it may be possible to put a deal into

---

11 Where an agreement is entered into contrary to Article 85(1) or Article 86 and the parties fail to notify the Commission, the Commission has the power to impose fines on each of the companies concerned of up to the greater of ECU 1,000,000 or 10 per cent of the relevant company's turnover in the previous year.

effect subject to appropriate notification, the parties will frequently make obtaining any required regulatory clearances a condition precedent to implementation of the joint venture.

In practice, the regulatory authority may not be able to enforce a total ban, particularly where the deal is international in character. In many cases, the objections will not be to the whole deal but to certain of its features, particularly in those cases mentioned above where industrial property rights, marketing rights, etc., are involved. The regulatory authority will then ask for the offending features to be removed and, if this is done then it will raise no objections to the deal. This procedure has become so widespread that it is quite usual for the parties to envisage such changes in drafting their initial agreements with a view to ensuring that the remainder of the deal stays in force undisturbed.

The European Commission has indeed developed a similar procedure in dealing with agreements that the parties have wrongly failed to notify and has allowed their confirmation subject to conditions. (See, for example, Feldmuehle AG and Stora Kopparbergs Bergslags AB (1982) *Community Press Release*, 23 February, 1982.)

An agreement which is not objected to or invalidated initially may still become objectionable later, possibly through the conduct of the parties which was not originally envisaged or fully disclosed in the original application for clearance.[12] In such a case, the controlling authority will normally have the right of review. Some bodies, particularly the European Commission, often approve a deal for a number of years only, after which it will have to be reviewed if extension is required. The European Commission also frequently stipulates the submission of regular reports. Any major change, such as the accession of a new participant, will reopen the case for review according to the individual legislation involved, as will negotiated changes to the agreements.

Conclusion

It is not within the scope of this book to do more than to indicate the matrix of considerations which may arise when the validity of a joint venture proposal is considered in relation to regulatory control over anti-competitive activities. It is particularly important for the negotiators and their advisers to look at all the territories in which they intend to

---

12 See, e.g. Brodley, *Antitrust Bulletin* (1976), p. 483.

conduct their operations or at least the principal territories, so that where appropriate they can obtain the requisite clearances in good time.

The literature relating in detail to the matters discussed in this chapter normally deals, of course, with one country or controlling body at a time, and any attempt to give a wide-ranging list of available literature would be outdated rapidly. Most of it will be found in articles rather than in complete books. American publications, even when they are concerned with international joint ventures, tend to focus on American anti-trust laws.[13] In view of the large number and variety of joint ventures involving US interests, the US Department of Justice first issued a set of guidelines called 'Antitrust and International Operations' in 1977. Since that time, the Guidelines have been revised twice, first in 1988 and then more recently in 1995. For those concerned specifically with joint ventures, the 1995 Guidelines are somewhat less helpful than the 1988 version in that they deal only with those principles of US anti-trust law which are generally relevant to international transactions and do not cover the attitude of the Department of Justice to joint ventures in any detail. However, for those unfamiliar with US anti-trust law the 1995 Guidelines do contain a useful summary of the main provisions in this area as well as the circumstances in which the US authorities will attempt to enforce US anti-trust law in relation to transactions outside the borders of the United States.

---

13 See, e.g. Young and Bradford pp. 61–64; but, more recently, Hawk looks at American involvement under EU law.

Appendix I

Check-list Relating to Agreements Covering Corporate Joint Ventures

I. General

1. Is a company/corporation the appropriate vehicle?   37–42
2. Applicable law and jurisdiction.
   - (a) Should agreements in 'international' cases be governed by law of domicile of joint venture (JV) or otherwise?   33–34
   - (b) Where more than one country is involved, should applicable law and jurisdiction coincide?   34
   - (c) In all cases, consider if arbitration is desirable. If yes, settle details.   34–35

   Note: Solution may differ between different agreements concerning the same JV.

   If parties normally use different languages and documents are produced in more than one language, agree which text governs.
3. When agreements drafted, check for enforceability under chosen law and also under mandatory provisions of other laws (e.g. restrictive practice legislation). Matters relating to the constitution of the corporation to be checked separately for conformity to appropriate corporation laws.   34, 41–42, 95–104

II. Agreements between Participants

A. Capital structure and constitution of corporation

1. Who will be the parties to the Shareholders' Agreement? Should the JV company itself be a party?   46

2. Define the business of the proposed joint venture in clear unambiguous terms. Is the business a specific project or a continuing business?   46

3. What authorizations, consents or licences are required to enable the JV company to commence operations?   91–93

4. Equity – other share capital – borrowings.
   (a) What will be the proportions of the parties' interests?   41
   (b) Issue of shares for non-cash contributions (technology; rights; input of existing business).   59–61
   (c) Use of separate classes of shares with equal rights to ensure common control.   48
   (d) Check no authorizations or consents required for investments.   91–92
   (e) Check taxation and other fiscal aspects.   84–88

5. Should shares be freely transferable? What limitation is desirable/permissible? Should transfer rights be limited to entire holding? If freely transferable to outsiders, consider pre-emption rights. What happens if pre-emption rights not taken up? Should the non-selling party have a second right to acquire the sale shares once the purchaser has been identified? Should a 'bring-along' provision be included? Should the parties have freedom to make intra-group transfers? Consider effect on agreements between transferor and JV. Consider providing for possible acquisition of a participant by an outside party and for his insolvency. Valuation procedure on transfer of shares? For other pre-emption rights, see Appendix III below. Should new shareholders be required to enter into a Deed of Adherence (i.e. a written undertaking in which they agree to be bound by the Shareholders' Agreement)? Consider transfer of loans/guarantees to incoming shareholder.   49–51

6. Will new shares be offered to shareholders pro rata to existing holdings? — 61
7. Consider:
   (a) List of topics requiring unanimity. — 51
   (b) Board composition and management set-up. — 56–57
   (c) Quorum for shareholders' and directors' meetings. — 48, 51
   (d) Similar arrangements for subsidiaries of JV. — 51–52
8. Deadlock: — 52–55
   (a) Limited solution available on profit distribution. — 52
   (b) Do parties wish to cover possible deadlock in advance? — 52
   (c) If so, consider:
       (i) casting vote; — 53
       (ii) arbitration; — 52–53
       (iii) outside director; — 53
       (iv) buy/sell options and/or liquidation; — 54
       (v) reference to Senior Management of the participants. — 53–54
   (d) Distinguish between management and legal disputes? — 52–53
9. Other reasons for discontinuance, e.g. asset deficiency. Consider effects of failure of one party to provide additional equity. — 61
10. Are there any specific circumstances which mean that put/call options are appropriate? — 63
11. Should the JV company be required to change its name if an existing participant sells its shares? — 74

B. Responsibilities of parties and restrictions on competition between the participants and between them and the JV

1. Should there be specific restraints on competition between: — 58
   (a) the participants themselves; and
   (b) the participants and the JV?
   If so, consider limitations.
2. Consider impact of competition law. — 95–104
3. Should after-acquisition of a competitive business be dealt with in advance? — 59

C. Matters for consideration in agreements between participants

1. Transfer to JV of existing business: 59–61
    (a) Valuation   aspects   including   choice   of   60
         currency(cies). Possible need for adjustment after
         ascertainment of value.
    (b) Should any warranties and/or indemnities be   60
         given by the contributor to the other parties or the
         Company.
    (c) Is any due diligence investigation required?   60
    (d) Consider taxation/fiscal implications of the busi-   84–86
         ness transfer.
    (e) Possible penalty for delay in making contribution.   61
2. Methods of financing and provision of further finance: 47–48,
    (a) Amount of finance initially required.   61–62
    (b) Ratio of equity to borrowings (if any). Consider
         tax aspects.
    (c) Will borrowings come from parties or from
         outside? Consider tax aspects. If from parties, will
         they be proportionate to equity shares? If not,
         interest and other terms need careful consider-
         ation. If from outside, will parties have to guaran-
         tee them? Jointly and severally for full amount?
         Consider putting limits of time and amount on
         loan and guarantee commitments.
    (d) Anticipate future financial requirements.   61–62
         Agree:
             (i) limits of future financial commitments;
            (ii) method of provision (equity-borrowing);
           (iii) conditions, if any, for such undertakings to
                  be activated.
         Consider possible exchange control problems.
    (e) Deal with situation where one or more parties will
         not/cannot join future financing. Does this block
         additional financing? If not, and money is put up
         by some but not all parties, are their equity stakes
         automatically adjusted? If so, what happens if a
         party's share becomes insignificant? Are put/call
         options activated or are the future control rights of
         that party reduced?

    (f) Where appropriate, deal with future provision of   64
parents' guarantees.

    (g) Is any other security available and/or appropriate?

  3. Trade with participants:

    (a) Define nature, level and duration of support   63
required.

    (b) Agree separate agreements between one or more   67–68
participants and JV as appendices to shareholders'
agreement.
(Also see III below.)

  4. What reporting information do the shareholders   64
require from the JV company?

  5. Consider statement as to JV company's accounting
policies.

  6. Other administrative matters such as location of
registered/principal office, choice of auditors, bankers,
etc.

  7. Mutual confidentiality and protection from hiring   65
other participants' staff.

  8. Profit distribution and repatriation of funds. Check on   62
remittance freedom in countries with exchange control. Protect against devaluation of local currency.

  9. Duration and termination: 73–74

    (a) will the duration be fixed? Alternatively, will
either party have the right to leave after a specified
period?

    (b) consider termination for 'default' related reasons.

    (c) are there any circumstances in which termination
will be automatic?

    (d) what will be the effect of termination on ancillary
contracts, e.g. premises, intellectual property
rights, supply/distribution agreements.

    (e) dissolution provision.

D. *Consider whether conditions precedent are appropriate
for example:*

    (a) governmental consents, licences and approvals;

    (b) approvals of third parties, e.g. lenders, landlords,
key contracts;

(c) availability of external finance.

III. Agreements Between One or More Participants and the JV

A. *Supply*

1. If JV depends on being supplied by one or more of the   68
   parties, consider terms (price, delivery, quality),
   period of commitment, mechanism for adjusting
   terms, and consequences of failure to supply.
   Consider fiscal effects of pricing policy.
2. If JV is to supply participants and this is crucial to its   68
   success, e.g. capacity utilization, define similar points
   as under 1 and penalties for failure to order and take
   delivery.
   If participants are in different countries, consider
   necessary variations in agreements to ensure
   enforceability.
   Consider restrictive practice impact of any long-term   97
   supply agreement.

B. *Services*

1. Requirement may cover, *inter alia*:   69
   (a)   Personnel on loan and/or management
         responsibility.
   (b)   Office facilities.
   (c)   Distribution facilities.
   (d)   Service facilities.
   (e)   Access to development effort.
2. Will any employees be transferred to the JV company
   on a permanent basis? If so, what will be the terms of
   their employment? Are there any wider implications of
   the transfer, e.g. pension arrangements, employee
   protection legislation, share option scheme? Will any
   employees be loaned to the company?

C. *Intellectual property*   69–71

1. If JV is intended to develop or acquire intellectual
   property, are participants meant to have privileged
   access? Consider their position if JV terminates. There
   may be need for special licensing arrangements at
   outset.

2. If JV depends upon access to participants' intellectual property, licences will be required. Territorial scope, degree of exclusivity, flow-back rights, rights to sublicence, right to improvements, etc., must be dealt with. Duration of agreements important.
3. All this has restrictive practice implications. In both of the above cases, situation after termination of JV should be addressed. There may be need for contingent licences to other participants.

IV. Governmental restraints

A. *Where appropriate, check rules on foreign investment*   91
(inward and outward)

B. *Check competition law and jurisdiction*

For this purpose consider:
1. What is the relevant market (field of operation,   95–96 territory).
2. Actual and prospective market shares of JV and all others.
3. Anti-competitive aspects of JV, including: 96–97
    (a) Implied undertakings.
    (b) Related agreements.
    (c) Post-JV situation.
    (d) Advantages or otherwise of alternative arrangements.

This check may involve several legal systems.

V. Termination of Joint Venture by New Agreement (e.g. buy-out)   73–74

A. *Is shareholding transferable or are preparatory steps required such as change in joint venture by-laws?*

B. *Is consideration fixed or dependent on valuation? Are governmental consents required?*

C. *Are special arrangements needed to cover:*
    1. status of and responsibility for employees;
    2. intellectual property;

3. services and supplies;
4. extended confidentiality undertakings.

D. *Which official bodies have to be notified and possibly give approval?*

For details go back over the appropriate parts of this check-list.

Appendix II

Typical Joint Venture Structures

A. Joint Research and Development (see Figure A)

X and Y enter a joint venture (JV) for joint development hitherto carried out by X alone. Both X and Y to be able to purchase development effort from the JV:

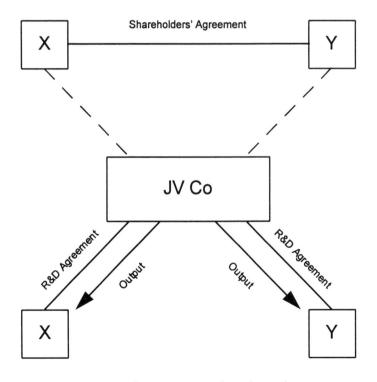

Figure A. Joint Research and Development

(a) Shareholders' Agreement (in this and subsequent examples, usually with draft memorandum and articles of association attached).
(b) Agreement for JV to purchase business from X.
(c) Research and development agreements between:
   (i)   JV and X;
   (ii) JV and Y.

B. Joint Distribution (see Figure B)

X and Y enter JV for exploiting in the territory of Y a product range to which both participants contribute product and know-how.

(a) Shareholders' Agreement.
(b) Technical assistance and licence agreements between:
   (i)   X and JV;
   (ii) Y and JV.

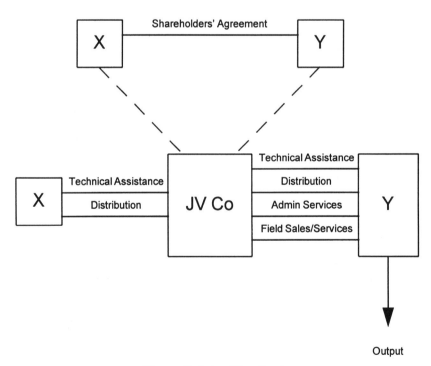

Figure B. Joint Distribution

(c)   Distribution agreements between:
  (i)   X and JV;
  (ii) Y and JV.
(d)   Agreement for administrative services between Y and JV.
(e)   Field sales and service agreement between Y and JV.

C. Income Access Structure (see Figure C)

1.   UK Parent and French Parent form a Netherlands JV Co to hold the business currently carried on by the UK Operating Companies and the French Operating Companies.

2.   Netherlands JV Co holds all the voting shares in UK Holding and French Holding, except that UK Parent and French Parent retain one share each in their 'local' companies. This 'income access' share

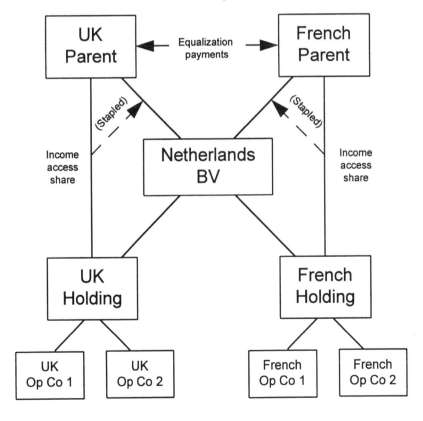

Figure C. Income Access Structure

entitles the holder to a dividend from the profits of the company in the holder's own tax jurisdiction, without routing it through the Netherlands JV Co.

3.   The income share is 'stapled' to the parent's holding in the Netherlands JV Co so that the shares 'cannot be held by separate shareholders. This is achieved through a restriction on ownership in the constitutional documents of UK Holding and French Holding.

4.   Since it is the intention that the UK and French organizations should be run as one business, there may be provision for payments between UK Parent and French Parent to 'equalize' their respective returns.

D. Independent Power Project (see Figure D)

1.   A, B and C (the 'sponsors') form a joint venture company to build, own and operate a power station in Host Country and subscribe for equity shares in JV Co.

2.   JV Co enters into:

(a)   a construction contract with the contractor to build the power station;

(b)   a power purchase agreement with a local utility (the 'power purchaser') under which the power purchaser agrees to purchase electricity at a price which enables JV Co's debt to be serviced and produces an agreed return for the sponsors;

(c)   a fuel supply contract with a local fuel supplier;

(d)   an operation and maintenance contract with an O & M contractor.

3.   The lenders agree to make loan finance available to JV Co to carry out the project under a credit agreement. JV Co assigns its entire interest in the power station and each of the agreements referred to in 2 above to the lenders as security.

4.   The government of Host Country agrees to support the project under a support agreement. The extent of the government's commitment under this agreement can vary from an undertaking

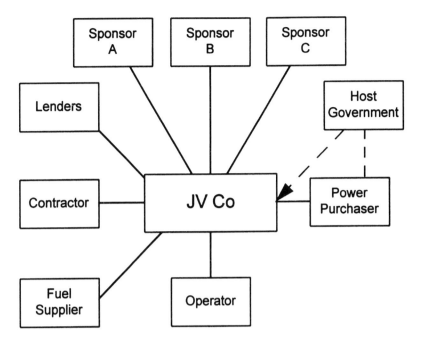

Figure D. Independent Power Project

not to revoke a particular licence JV Co requires to a full guarantee of the power purchaser's obligations.

E. Management Buy-Out (see Figure E)

1. The management form a special purpose company to acquire the business of Target and its subsidiaries.

2. The management enter into long-term service contracts with JV Co to ensure that their services continue to be available to the business.

3. The management and the venture capital fund enter into a Subscription and Shareholders' Agreement under which each agrees to subscribe for an agreed number of shares in JV Co (which may be of various classes).

4. The lenders agree to make loan finance available to JV Co for the acquisition of Target under a credit agreement.

5. JV Co acquires Target under a share sale agreement from the vendor.

6.   Each of JV Co, Target and its subsidiaries create security over their assets in favour of lenders.

Note

In most jurisdictions there are restrictions on the ability of Target and its subsidiaries to give security in connection with finance to assist the purchase of their own shares, which will have to be borne in mind when structuring the transaction.

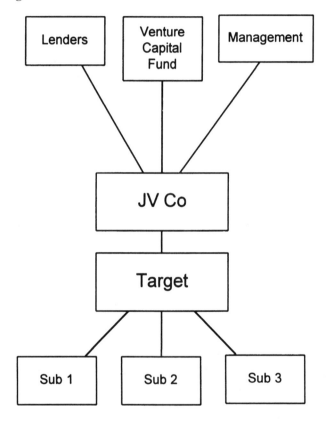

Figure E. Management Buy-Out

Appendix III

Sample Clauses

A. Minority Protection

The following is an example of a clause requiring unanimity at a board meeting:

'The parties shall procure that none of the following actions shall be taken in relation to the Joint Company unless prior approval has been given by a unanimous resolution of the Board passed at a duly constituted board meeting [at which at least one [A Director] and at least one [B Director] is present]:

   (i)   any change in the nature or scope of the Company's business;
   (ii)   any amendment to the Company's constitutional documents;
   (iii) a change of the Company's name;
   (iv)   any loans to or borrowings by the Company in excess of £[   ];
   (v)   the giving of any guarantee or other security by the Company or any transaction having similar effect;
   (vi)   the making of any loans by the Company;
   (vii) approval of the Company's business plans and budgets;
   (viii) any capital expenditure in excess of the figure authorized in the latest budget approved under (vii) above;
   (ix)   the declaration of dividends other than as agreed in the Shareholders' Agreement;
   (x)   the formation of subsidiaries or joint ventures;
   (xi)   the employment and removal of key management;
   (xii) any changes in the share or stock structure of the Company including the creation, allotment or issue of new shares, any reduction in capital, the grant of options over any of the Company's shares;
   (xiii) the commencement and conduct of material litigation;

    (xiv)   the entering into or termination of material contracts, i.e. any contract (aa) between the Company and one of the shareholders; or (bb) at a consideration in excess of £[   ] or for a duration in excess of [   ] years; or (cc) otherwise than on 'arm's length' terms; or (dd) other than in the course of the Company's ordinary business;

    (xv)   material acquisitions or disposals;

    (xvi)   the appointment or removal of the Company's auditors;

    (xvii)   the adoption of the Company's accounting policies and any changes to them;

    (xviii)   the establishment of a pension scheme or other scheme for the benefit of the Company's employees;

    (xix)   material transactions relating to intellectual property rights;

    (xx)   [any other transaction which is likely to have a material effect on the Company's business, e.g. approval of an application for a key licence or tender for major contract(s)];

    (xxi)   a merger or amalgamation of the Company with another Company;

    (xxii)   the commencement of a winding-up of the Company or cessation of the Company's business.'

Notes

1.   It may often be advisable to provide for certain 'reserved matters' to be decided by the parties themselves rather than the directors they have nominated (see p. 56).

2.   Where it is likely that the Joint Company will have subsidiaries, the clause should be so worded as to ensure that subsidiaries have to comply with the same restrictions (see pp. 51–52).

    There may be provision to adjust value limits periodically for inflation, etc.

B. Russian Roulette

The agreement must define in which circumstances the following clause operates. It may be used in case of a deadlock that has not been remedied over a stated period of time but can also apply in a number of other situations.

    '(a)   A notice of termination given by either party (in this and the remaining paragraphs of this article called "X") to the other (called "Y") under the above clause shall contain either:

      (i)   an offer by X to buy all of Y's shares in the Company at a specified price; or

      (ii)   an offer by X to sell all X's shares in the Company to Y at a specified price.

(b)   Within 30 days of receipt of such notice Y shall by notice in writing to X either:

      (i)   accept the offer contained in X's notice; or

      (ii)   where X has offered to buy Y's shares, make a counter-offer to buy all of X's shares in the Company at the price specified in X's offer; or

      (iii) where X has offered to sell its shares in the Company to Y, make a counter-offer to sell all of its shares in the Company to X at the price specified in X's offer.

(c)   If Y gives no notice to X within the time stipulated in paragraph (b) above, Y shall be treated as having accepted the offer made by X under paragraph (a) and shall accordingly be bound to accept or to make, as the case may be, a transfer of shares in the Company at the price specified in that offer.

(d)   X shall be bound to accept any counter-offer made by Y in accordance with paragraph (b) above and shall accordingly be bound to accept or to make, as the case may be, a transfer of shares in the Company at the price specified in that offer.

(e)   Each party hereto shall co-operate to obtain all necessary governmental and other consents for the implementation of the provisions of this clause.

(f)   Each party hereto irrevocably appoints the other as its attorney for the purposes of executing a transfer of shares which the appointing party is bound to make under paragraph (c) and (d) above.'

C. Put and Call Options

' 1.   X hereby grants to Y an option to require X to purchase ('the Put Option') and Y grants to X an option to purchase ('the Call Option'), Y's entire interest in Shares in the company (the 'Option Shares') subject to the following terms and conditions.

2.   Y may exercise the Put Option by 30 days' written notice to X given at any time during the period commencing on [   ] and ending on [   ].

3.   X may exercise the Call Option by 30 days' written notice to Y given at any time during the period commencing on [   ] and ending on [   ].

4. The price payable for the Option Shares under either the Put Option or the Call Option ('the Option Price') shall be [the greater of]:

    (a) [   ] times the average Net Tangible Assets; or
    (b) [   ] times the average After Tax Earnings;

    For the last three Financial Years of the Company prior to the date of the exercise of the relevant Option as certified by the auditors of the Company in writing.

    In this clause 4:

    (i)   'Net Tangible Assets' shall mean the fixed assets and current assets of the Company (including, for the avoidance of doubt, both current and deferred tax liabilities);
    (ii) 'After Tax Earnings' shall mean the actual after-tax earnings of the Company before the payment of dividends (including any extraordinary profits and losses as disclosed in the audited accounts);
    (iii) unless otherwise agreed by each of the Parties, the same accounting principles and policies shall be applied for the purpose of this calculation for all periods up to the exercise of the Put Option, or the Call Option as the case may be.

5. Upon expiry of a notice of exercise of the Put Option or the Call Option (as the case may be):

    (a) X shall pay or procure payment of the Option Price to Y;
    (b) Y shall deliver to X a duly completed transfer or transfers in respect of the Option Shares in favour of X or as X may direct together with the relative share certificates; and
    (c) subject to payment of any stamp duty payable on the transfer the Parties shall procure that the said transfer is registered in the Company's books.

6. The Option Shares shall be sold free from all liens, charges and encumbrances and with all rights attached thereto at the date of exercise of the relevant Option.'

Notes

1. Where the joint venture company has subsidiaries, the option price should be calculated by reference to the consolidated net tangible assets or after tax earnings of the group.

2. Where there are outstanding loans by the vendor (Y in the above example) to the joint venture company the clause may provide for these loans to be transferred to the purchaser along with the option shares.

3. Where governmental or other consents or approvals to the change of ownership are required, the transfer would have to be deferred until such contents or approvals are obtained. In such a case it is usual to provide that the parties should co-operate in procuring the requisite consents or approvals.

4. The existence of put or call options can have a significant impact on the joint venture company's status for tax purposes (see p. 85).

D. Dividends

It may be possible to lay down in the agreement a payout ratio in such a way that failure by one party to comply would put it in breach of the agreement. In case this is not considered adequate, there follows a rather more complicated arrangement.

1. *Articles of Association of Joint Company*

'Subject to the limitations set forth in this article, holders of Class A Stock shall be entitled to receive dividends declared by the A Directors, and holders of Class B Stock shall be entitled to receive dividends declared by the B Directors. In furtherance of the foregoing:

(a) There shall be two committees of the board of directors which shall have power to declare and authorize the payment of dividends by the Company. One committee shall be composed solely of one or more A Directors (which committee shall be appointed by the A Directors or by a sole remaining A Director), which shall be designated the Class A Dividend Committee, and shall have power to declare and authorize the payment of dividends on the Class A Stock. The other committee, which shall be designated the Class B Dividend Committee, shall be composed solely of one or more B Directors (which committee shall be appointed by the B Directors or a sole remaining B Director) and shall have power to declare and authorize the payment of dividends on the Class B Stock. In each fiscal year of the Company, each Dividend Committee, at any meeting of the board of directors (even if there is not a quorum of the board of directors) for which proper notice has been given and at which at least one member of such

Dividend Committee shall be present in person or by telephone conference, shall have authority to declare dividends on the Class A Stock or the Class B Stock, as the case may be, at any time and from time to time after the first meeting of the board of directors after receipt of the consolidated audited financial statements of the Company and its subsidiaries for the immediately preceding fiscal year (or if such meeting shall not have occurred within 150 days following the end of the immediately preceding fiscal year of the Company, at any time on or following such 150th day) but prior to the 60th day preceding the end of the then current fiscal year of the Company; provided that the aggregate amount of dividends declared by either of such Dividend Committees in any fiscal year of the Company on its class of stock shall not exceed: (a) the product of the sum of the adjusted net profits (as defined in paragraph (c) of this article) for the first and second fiscal years preceding the fiscal year in which such dividends are declared, times a fraction, the numerator of which shall be the number of shares of such class ("A" or "B") outstanding at the time of such declaration and the denominator of which shall be the number of shares of common stock of all classes outstanding on such date, minus (b) any dividends declared by such Dividend Committee in the immediately preceding fiscal year prior to such immediately preceding fiscal year. For purposes of clause (b) of the proviso to the foregoing sentence, dividends declared by either Dividend Committee in every fiscal year shall first be allocated to the adjusted net profits for the second preceding fiscal year and then to the immediately preceding fiscal year.

(b)   The board of directors of the Company shall, at the first properly constituted meeting of such board after receipt of the consolidated audited financial statement of the Company and its subsidiaries for the immediately preceding fiscal year (and in any event within 150 days after the end of such year), consider setting apart out of any of the funds of the Company available for dividends a reserve or reserves for any proper purpose (and may abolish any such reserves), but only as herein provided. The amount, if any, which is set aside out of consolidated earnings from such year by unanimous vote of all members of the board of directors who are present at a properly constituted meeting (or, in the alternative, which is set aside by written consent of all members of such board) shall be called the Reserved Amount. If, for any reason, an amount is not so agreed upon the requisite unanimous approval within 150 days after the end of the previous fiscal year, the Reserved Amount for such year shall be zero.

Without the approval of all the members who are present at a properly constituted meeting of the board of directors of the Company or the written consent of all the members of such board of directors, there shall not be established any reserves out of any of the funds of the Company available for dividends, nor shall any amounts in excess of the par value of the outstanding shares of stock of the Company be allocated to the capital account of the Company. In no event may any Dividend Committee take any of the actions described in the preceding sentence.

(c) The "Adjusted net profits" for any fiscal year shall mean the consolidated net profits of the Company and its subsidiaries for such year as reported in the audited consolidated financial statements of the Company and its subsidiaries for such year, with the following adjustments: . . .

(d) If any dividend shall be declared by either Dividend Committee, such Dividend Committee shall fix the date such dividend shall be payable (which shall be a date not less than 30 nor more than 90 days after such dividend is declared). Any dividend validly declared by either Dividend Committee shall be an obligation of the company and the officers (subject to any instructions from the board of directors not inconsistent with such declaration) shall take such actions not contrary to law as shall be necessary and appropriate to pay such dividend.

(e) On any liquidation or dissolution of the Company all shares of common stock (whether Class A Stock or Class B Stock) shall be treated equally, except that if for any class of common stock of the Company the sum of all dividends paid on all shares of such class for all fiscal years of the Company divided by the average of the number of shares of such class outstanding at the end of each fiscal year of the Company shall exceed the sum of all dividends paid on all shares of the other class for all fiscal years of the Company divided by the average of the number of shares of such other class outstanding at the end of each fiscal year of the Company, then there shall first be distributed (to the extent available) pro rata with respect to each share of such other class at the time outstanding an amount equal to such excess and the balance, if any, shall be distributed pro rata with respect to each share of the Company's common stock.'

2. *This is covered in the Shareholders' Agreement as follows:*

'(a) X agrees that, if Y (and its subsidiaries) shall fail to receive any dividend validly declared by the Class B Dividend Committee of the Joint Company in accordance with the Joint Company's articles of association within 60 days after such dividend is so declared as the result of the failure of any A Directors of the Joint Company to co-operate, to the fullest extent permitted by law and the Joint Company's articles of association, in taking such actions (including causing all subsidiaries and sub-subsidiaries of the Joint Company to dividend their full earnings to the Joint Company) as may be necessary to enable and cause the Joint Company to pay such dividend, X shall pay to Y (and its subsidiaries) an amount equal to the dividend which Y and any subsidiary of Y would have been entitled to receive had all of the A Directors so co-operated (minus any amount which, had the Joint Company paid such dividend, the Joint Company would have been required by law to withhold on account of any taxes with respect to the payment of such dividend).

(b)   Y agrees that, if X (and its subsidiaries) shall fail to receive any dividend validly declared by the Class A Dividend Committee of the Joint Company in accordance with the Joint Company's articles of association within 60 days after such dividend is so declared as the result of the failure of any B Directors of the Joint Company to co-operate, to the fullest extent permitted by law and the Joint Company's articles of association, in taking such actions (including causing all subsidiaries and sub-subsidiaries of the Joint Company to dividend their full earnings to the Joint Company) as may be necessary to enable and cause the Joint Company to pay such dividend, Y shall pay to X (and its subsidiaries) an amount equal to the dividend which X and any subsidiary of X would have been entitled to receive had all of the B Directors so co-operated (minus any amount which, had the Joint Company paid such dividend, the Joint Company would have been required by law to withhold on account on any taxes with respect to the payment of such dividend).

(c)   In the event that either X or Y is required to pay any amount to the other pursuant to this section with respect to the failure by the Joint Company to pay any dividend, the rights of the party receiving such amount to receive the dividend with respect to which such payment was made (but not such party's right to receive any other dividends) shall, to the extent of the amount received from the other party, be subrogated to the party paying such amount.'

Note:

The freedom of the A Directors and the B Directors to declare dividends under this clause is subject to the overriding consideration that they must at all times act in the best interests of the Company. Thus, if business considerations require the profits of a particular year to be retained, the declaration of a dividend under this provision may be unlawful.

E. Share Transfers

Restrictions on share transfers can vary from absolute prohibition to right of first refusal (see pp. 49–51). The following somewhat elaborate set of conditions covers an arrangement between two major companies.

'Restrictions on Transfer of Shares

(a) During a period ending at the later of, (i) seven (7) years after the date of execution of this agreement or (ii) two (2) years after either X or Y shall have given written notice (whether such notice shall be given before or after the end of the seven year period referred to in clause (i)) to the other of a desire to dispose of any shares of the Joint Company stock, no shares of the Joint Company or any interest therein may be sold, distributed, transferred, assigned or otherwise disposed of, directly or indirectly, by either X or Y, except with the written consent of the other party with specific reference to this section of this agreement.

(b) Following the expiration of the period described in section (a), each of X or Y may sell for cash all, but not part only, of the shares of the Joint Company owned by it subject to the rights of first refusal and of participation set forth in section (c) of this agreement.

(c) X and Y shall each have a right of first refusal with respect to the shares of the Joint Company common stock of the other and a right of participation with respect to any sale of the shares of the other, which rights shall be exercised in accordance with the following provisions:

    (i) The shareholder desiring to sell all of its shares (the "Offeror") shall first offer to the other shareholder (the "Offeree") the following options: (a) to buy such shares from the Offeror at the same price less_____per cent and upon the same terms and conditions as the Offeror has been offered and is willing to accept from a third party in a bona fide, arm's length transaction in which the Offeror did not and does not have any direct or indirect beneficial ownership interest in such third party with a value exceeding_____or_____per cent of the voting stock (or other equity interests) of such third party, or (b) to sell all but not less than all of the Joint Company shares owned by such Offeree to such third party on the same terms and conditions as the sale by the Offeror.

(ii)   The offer by the Offeror to the Offeree shall: (a) disclose all the details pertaining to any such proposed transaction with a third party, including the price, terms and conditions and the name and address of the third party to whom the Offeror is prepared to sell such shares and (b) state that such third party has agreed, for the benefit of the Offeree, to purchase all shares of the Joint Company common stock owned by the Offeree. If the Offeree elects to exercise its right to purchase the Offeror's shares of the Joint Company stock, it shall give written notice thereof to the Offeror within sixty (60) days after receipt of such offer from the Offeror, and the purchase of such shares shall be closed at the general offices of the Joint Company (or at any other mutually agreeable place as may be designated by the Offeree) within ninety (90) days after the Offeree's notice of such election to the Offeror and any necessary governmental reviews, consents or approvals have occurred, or at any other mutually agreeable time.

(iii)   If the Offeree elects to participate in such sale by selling all its shares in the Joint Company to such third party, it shall give written notice thereof to the Offeror and such third party within sixty (60) days after receipt of such offer from the Offeror, in which case the Offeror shall not sell its shares to such third party unless such third party purchases all of the Offeree's shares, at the same time, and on the same terms and conditions, as the Offeror's shares are purchased.

(iv)   If the Offeree does not elect to exercise its right to purchase the shares or to sell its shares within such sixty (60) day period, the Offeror may sell Offeror's shares to the third party, provided that such sale is made within ninety (90) days after the expiration of the sixty (60) day first refusal period, at a price and upon terms and conditions not more favourable to such third party or to the Offeror than those who were first disclosed to the Offeree; and provided that the third party agrees to be bound by the terms of this agreement, in which event this agreement shall continue in effect among the shareholders; provided that such third party shall be bound by, and entitled to the benefits of, this section (c), except that such third party shall not be entitled to the benefits of the_____per cent discount provided for in clause (i) of this section (c).

(v)   Within thirty (30) days after the consummation of any such sale to such third party, the Offeror shall furnish to the Offeree and to the Joint Company: (a) if the Offeree shall not have participated in such sale, an agreement of such third party agreeing to be bound by the terms of this agreement (and acknowledging that such third party shall be bound by, and entitled to the benefits of, this section (c), except that such third party shall not be entitled to the benefits of the _____per cent discount provided for in clause (i) of this section (c) and (b) whether or not the Offeree shall have participated in such sale, an affidavit of the Offeror setting forth: (x) the name and address of the third party to whom such shares were sold; (y) the price and terms and conditions upon which such shares were sold; and (z) a statement to the effect that such sale was made to a third party in which the Offeror did not and does not have a direct or indirect beneficial ownership interest with a value in excess of_____or constituting in excess of_____per cent of the voting stock (or other equity interests) of such third party. The Joint Company shall not register such sale on the books of the Joint Company and shall not deliver a stock certificate to such third party, until such agreement (if required) and such affidavit are so delivered.'

Bibliography

Adler, S. and Morris, D., 'The risks and rewards of plunging into collaborative Ventures', *The Financial Times*, 15 November 1982.

American Jurisprudence, Vol. 46, second edition (The Lawyers' Co-operative Publishing Co., Rochester N.Y., 1969).

Baker, R.J. and Cary, W. L., *Cases and Materials on Corporations*, fourth edition (The Foundation Press, Mineola N.Y., 1986).

Beamish, P. W., *Multinational Joint Ventures in Developing Countries* (Routledge, 1988).

Beamish, P. W. and Banks, J. C., 'Equity Joint Ventures and the Theory of the Multinational Enterprise', *Journal of International Business Studies*, Vol. 18 (Summer 1987), pp. 1–16.

Bellamy, Ch., and Child, G., *Common Market Law of Competition*, fourth edition (Sweet & Maxwell, 1993).

Berg, S. V., Duncan, J., and Friedman, P., *Joint Venture Strategies and Corporate Innovation* (Oelgeschlager, Gunn & Hain, Cambridge, Mass., 1982).

Berg, S. V., and Friedman, P., 'Joint Ventures in American Industry', Parts I–III, *Mergers and Acquisitions*, Vol. 13 (1978/9).

—— 'Corporate courtship and successful Joint Ventures', *California Management Review*, Vol. 22 (1980), pp. 85 *et seq.*

Blanden, M., 'Joint Ventures and consortium banks – why banks choose to work together', *Banker* (March 1981), pp. 93 *et seq.*

Booz-Allen and Hamilton, *A Practical Guide to Alliances* (Los Angeles).

Boulton, A. H., *Business Consortia* (Sweet & Maxwell, 1961).

Brelsford, J. F., 'Apparent authority and the Joint Venture: narrowing the scope of agency between business associates', *University of California Davis Law Review*, Vol. 13 (1980), pp. 831 *et seq.*

Broden, T. F. and Scanlan, A. L., 'The legal status of Joint Venture corporations', *Vanderbilt Law Review*, Vol. 11 (1957/8), pp. 673 *et seq.*

Brodley, J. F., 'The legal status of Joint Ventures under the antitrust laws: a summary assessment', *Antitrust Bulletin*, Vol. 21 (1976), pp. 453 *et seq.*

—— 'Joint ventures and anti-trust policy', *Harvard Law Review*, Vol. 95 (1982), pp. 1523 *et seq.*

Brooke, M. Z. and Remmers, H. L., *The Strategy of Multinational Enterprise – Organisation and Finance*, second edition (Pitman, 1978).

Brown, J. T., 'International Joint Venture contracts in English law', *Droit et Pratique du Commerce International*, Vol. 5 (1979), pp. 193 *et seq.*

Cavitch, Z., *Business Organisations with Tax Planning* (Matthew Bender, New York), para. 41.05.

Claydon, J.-M., 'Joint Ventures – an analysis of commission decisions', *ECLR* 1986, pp. 151 *et seq.*

Contractor, F. C. and Lorange, P., 'Why should firms co-operate? The strategy and economics basis for co-operative ventures', in *Co-operation Strategies in International Business*, Contractor, F. C. and Lorange, P. (eds.) (Lexington Books, Toronto, 1988).

Cossette, P. A., 'Les groupements momentanés d'entreprises (joint ventures): nature juridique en droit civil et en common law', *Revue du Barreau* (Quebec) Vol. 44 (1984) pp. 463 *et seq.*

Dabin, L. (ed.) *et al.*, 'Accords de coopération inter-entreprises pour la réalisation de marchés internationaux', *Droit et Pratique du Commerce International*, Vol. 5 (1979), pp. 337 *et seq.*

Doran, N., *Taxation of Corporate Joint Ventures* (Butterworth, 1993).

Duncan, W. D. (ed.), *Joint Ventures Law in Australia* (Federation Press, 1993).

Dunning, J. H., *The Globalization of Business* (Routledge, 1993).

Ehinger, K., 'Vertragsrahmen des industriellen internationalen Equity Joint Venture', *Heidelberg Colloquium 1986 on The Complex Long-Term Contract* (C. F. Müller, 1987), pp. 187 *et seq.* (with English summary).

Ellison, J. and King, E. (eds.), *Joint Ventures in Europe – A collaborative study* (Butterworth, 1991).

Fine, F. L., *Mergers and Joint Ventures in Europe – The Law and Policy of the EEC*, second edition (Kluwer, 1994).

Finnen, M. W., 'Imposition of a constructive trust based upon a breach of a fiduciary duty in Joint Venture Situations', *South Texas Law Journal*, Vol. 21 (1981), pp. 229 *et seq.*

Foster, G., 'The Joint Venture gambit', *Management Today* (February 1973), pp. 74 *et seq.*

Franko, L. G., *Joint Venture Survival in Multinational Corporations* (Praeger Publishers, New York, 1971).

—— 'The art of choosing an American Joint Venture partner', *The Multinational Company in Europe – Some Key Problems* (Praeger Publishers, New York, 1972) Brooke and Remmers (eds.) pp. 65 *et seq.*

Friedmann, W. G. and Beguin, J-P., *Joint International Business Ventures in Developing Countries* (Columbia University Press, 1971).

Friedmann, W. G. and Kalmanoff, G., *Joint International Business Ventures* (Columbia University Press, 1961).

Gavin, M. K., 'Protecting the entrepreneur: special drafting concerns for international Joint Venture contracts', *University of California Davis Law Review*, Vol. 14 (1980/1981), pp. 1001 *et seq.*

Gillespie, I. (ed.), *Joint Ventures – A Eurostudy Special Report* (Eurostudy Publishing Company Ltd., 1990).

Goetz, G. J., and Scott, R. E., 'Principles of relational contracts', *Virginia Law Review*, Vol. 67 (1981), pp. 1089 *et seq.*

Gorton, L., 'Joint Ventures in shipping law', *JBL* 1978, pp. 238 *et seq.*

Gullander, S., 'Joint Ventures and corporate strategy', *Columbia Journal of World Business* (Spring 1976), pp. 102 *et seq.*

—— 'Joint Ventures in Europe – Determinants of entry', *1–2 International Studies of Management and Organizations*, Vol. 6 (1976), pp. 85 *et seq.*

Hale, G. E., 'Joint Ventures: collaborative subsidiaries and the antitrust laws', *Virginia Law Review*, Vol. 42 (1956), pp. 927 *et seq.*

Hall, R. D., *The International Joint Venture* (Praeger Publishers, New York, 1984).

Harvard Law Review, 'Joint venture corporations: drafting the corporate papers', (1964/1965), pp. 393 *et seq.*

Herzfeld, E., 'Co-operation agreements in corporate Joint Ventures', *JBL* (1983), pp. 121 *et seq.*

—— 'Typical areas of conflicts of interest in Joint Ventures', *Heidelberg Colloquium 1986 on The Complex Long-Term Contract* (C. F. Müller, 1987), pp. 199 *et seq.*

—— and Hadley, R., *Contracting and Subcontracting for Overseas Projects* (Graham & Trotman, 1988).

Hlavacek, J. D., Dovey, B. H. and Biondo, J. J., 'Tie small business technology to marketing power', *Harvard Business Review*, Vol. 55 (January/February 1977), pp. 106 *et seq.*

Hlavacek, J. D., and Thompson, V. A., 'The Joint Venture approach to technology utilisation', *IEEE Transactions on Engineering Management*, Vol. 23, No. 1 (February 1976), pp. 35 *et seq.*

Inkpen, A., *The Management of International Joint Ventures* (Routledge, 1995).

Joint Ventures Practice Manual, loose-leaf (Legal & Commercial Publishing, London).

Jowitt, *Dictionary of English Law*, second edition (Sweet & Maxwell, 1977), p. 1016.

Killing, J. P., *Strategies for Joint Venture Success* (Croom Helm, 1983).

Kolde, E. J., *International Business Enterprise* (Prentice-Hall Inc., 1968), pp. 259 *et seq.*

—— *The Multinational Company* (D. C. Heath & Co., 1974), pp. 127 *et seq.*

Lang, J. Temple, 'Joint Ventures under the EEC Treaty rules on competition', *Irish Jurist* (1977), pp. 15 *et seq.*; (1978), pp. 132 *et seq.*; and (1980), pp. 13 *et seq.*

Larcier, R., 'Y a-t-il un mystère des "Joint Ventures"', *Analyse Financière* (1983), Vol. 54, pp. 94 *et seq.*

—— 'Les "Joint Ventures", vecteurs de diversification', *Mélanges en l'honneur de Edwin Borschberg* (1986) (Editions Universitaires Fribourg).

Lewis, T., 'The benefits of alliance', *Mergers and Acquisitions International* (January 1989), pp. xxxv *et seq.*

Mercadal, B. and Janin, P., *Le contrats de coopération inter-entreprises* (Editions Juridiques Lefebvre, Paris, 1974).

Mok, M. R., 'The jointly owned subsidiary ("Joint Venture") and Article 85 of the EEC Treaty', *European Competition Policy* (Leiden, 1973), pp. 120 *et seq.*

Morris, J. M., *Joint Ventures: An Accounting, Tax and Administrative Guide* (Wiley, 1987).

Müller-Gugenberger, C. H., 'Principes d'organisation de coopération d'entreprises en droit allemand', *Droit et Pratique du Commerce International*, Vol. 3 (1977), pp. 475 *et seq.*

Nightingale, C., *Joint Ventures* (Longman, 1990).

Ohmae, K., *Triad Power* (Macmillan, 1985).

Paillusseau, J. and Lecerf, M., 'Les groupements de coopération interentreprises (GIE et GEC)', *Droit et Pratique du Commerce International*, Vol. 3 (1977), pp. 139 *et seq.*

Pfeffer, J. and Nowak, P., 'Joint Ventures and inter-organisational interdependence', *Administrative Science Quarterly* (1976), pp. 398 *et seq.*

Radin, *Law Dictionary*, second edition (Oceana Publications Inc., New York, 1970), pp. 174, 361.

Reymond, C., 'Le contrat de "Joint Venture"' in *'Innominatverträge'*, *Festgabe für W. R. Schluep* (Schulthess, 1988).

Ritter, L. and Overbury, C., 'An attempt at a practical approach to Joint Ventures under the EEC Rules on Competition', *CMLR*, Vol. 14 (1977), pp. 601 *et seq.*

Roulac, S. E., 'Structuring the Joint Venture', *Mergers and Acquisitions* (Spring 1980), pp. 4 *et seq.*

Schmitthoff, C. M., 'Joint Ventures in Europe' in *Commercial Operations in Europe*, Goode, R. M., and Simmonds, K. R. (eds.), (University of London, 1978), pp. 332 *et seq.*

Segall, H. A., and Sirkin, M. S., 'Providing for withdrawal from a Joint Venture', *The Practical Lawyer*, Vol. 28 (1982), pp. 75 *et seq.*

Walker, R. and Tank, A., *Making Alliances Work – Lessons from Companies' Successes and Mistakes* (Business International Limited).

Way, P. (ed.), *Taxation of Joint Ventures* (Longman, 1994).

Wetter, J. G., 'A multi-party arbitration scheme for international Joint Ventures', *Arbitration International* (1987), pp. 2 *et seq.*

Words and Phrases, US Edition, Vol. 23 (West Publishing Co.), p. 227.

Young, G. R., and Bradford, S. Jr., *Joint Ventures: planning and action* (Financial Executives Research Foundation, New York, 1977).

Zaphiriou, G. A., 'Methods of co-operation between independent enterprises (Joint Ventures)', *American Journal of Comparative Law*, Vol. 26 (1978), Supplement, pp. 245 *et seq.*

Zweigert, K. and von Hoffmann, B., 'Zur internationalen Joint Venture', *Festschrift für M. Luther* (Ch. Beck, 1976), pp. 203 *et seq.*

Index